WRITERS AND THEIR WORK

ISOBEL ARMSTRONG
General Editor

GRAHAM SWIFT

Photograph © Eamonn McCabe

GRAHAM SWIFT

GRAHAM SWIFT

Peter Widdowson

First published in 2006 by Northcote House Publishers Ltd, Horndon, Tavistock, Devon, PL19 9NQ, United Kingdom.
Tel: +44 (0) 1822 810066 Fax: +44 (0) 1822 810034.

British Library Cataloguing-in-Publication Data
A catalogue record for this book is available from the British Library

ISBN 0-7463-1104-4 hardcover
ISBN 0-7463-1012-9 paperback

Typeset by PDQ Typesetting, Newcastle-under-Lyme
Printed and bound in the United Kingdom
by Athenaeum Press Ltd., Gateshead, Tyne & Wear

For all those English students at the
University of Gloucestershire who over the years
have read Graham Swift with me.

Contents

Acknowledgements

There is no better way to get to know an author's work than to teach it. The pleasurable experience over a number of years of studying *Waterland* with second-year students and offering soon-to-graduate third-year students a special option on Graham Swift's fiction is the foundation on which the present volume rests. As the dedication makes clear, therefore, my principal debt is to all those students whose enthusiastic engagement with the novels sustained mine.

A short synoptic version of this book appeared as an essay, 'The Novels of Graham Swift', in Rick Rylance and Judy Simons (eds), *Literature in Context* (Basingstoke and New York: Palgrave, 2001), and much reduced versions of Chapter 3 on *Out of This World* have previously been published in my 'Newstories: Fiction, History and the Modern World', *Critical Survey*, 7/1 (1995), 3–17 and in chapter 5 of my *Literature* (New Critical Idiom; London and New York: Routledge, 1999), 159–64.

Biographical Outline

1949	Graham Swift born on 4 May in south London (borders of Sydenham and Catford).
1950s	Swift family moves to Croydon while GS is still very young. Grows up sharply aware of his father's wartime service as a naval fighter pilot and of the physical evidence of the Second World War all around.
1954–60	Attends Croydon Grammar School. Wins scholarship to Dulwich College.
1960–7	Attends Dulwich College. Decides to become a writer.
1967–70	Attends Queens' College, Cambridge. First short stories published in college journal, *Solstice*. Graduates with a First in English in 1970.
1970–3	Undertakes a Ph.D. on 'The Role of the City in Nineteenth-Century English Literature' at the University of York, but actually spends his time teaching himself to write. Meets Candice Rodd, his long-term partner.
1974	Abandons Ph.D. for a year in Greece, teaching English in Volos and writing his first (unpublished) novel.
1975	Returns to London, where he begins living with Candice Rodd (journalist and editor) in Clapham.
1975–82	Supports himself with part-time jobs (security guard, farm-worker, but principally teaching in Further Education Colleges in London). Writes and begins to publish short stories in collections (*New Stories*, *Winter's Tales*, and *Firebird*, a Penguin

	anthology of contemporary writing) and literary journals (*Punch*, *Stand Magazine*, and especially the *London Magazine*, edited by Alan Ross – see 1982).
1980	First published novel, *The Sweet Shop Owner*, appears to favourable reviews.
1981	Second novel, *Shuttlecock*, published.
1982	Volume of short stories, *Learning to Swim*, published by London Magazine Editions.
1983	*Waterland* published to great acclaim: short-listed for the Booker Prize; wins the *Guardian* Fiction Award, the Winifred Holtby Memorial Prize, and the Italian Premio Grinzane Cavour. Swift included in the *Granta Best of Young British Novelists* collection. Film, 1992. Now able to write full-time.
1985	Edits and introduces (with David Profumo) *The Magic Wheel: An Anthology of Fishing in Literature* (Swift's favourite pastime is reported to be fishing).
1988	*Out of This World* published.
1992	*Ever After* published: wins the Prix du Meilleur Livre Etranger in France. Steven Gyllenhaal's film of *Waterland*, starring Jeremy Irons and Sinéad Cusack.
1996	*Last Orders* published: wins Booker Prize. Film, 2001.
1996 7	John Frow, Professor of English at the University of Queensland, writes to the *Australian*'s 'Review of Books' pointing out that *Last Orders* is 'almost identical' to William Faulkner's *As I Lay Dying* (1930), thus implicitly accusing Swift of plagiarism. Reported in the *Guardian* (10 March 1997) and the *Independent on Sunday* (16 March 1997), provoking a furious response, mainly by supporters of Swift.
2001	Fred Schepsi's film of *Last Orders*, starring Michael Caine, Tom Courtenay, David Hemmings, Bob Hoskins, Helen Mirren and Ray Winstone.
2003	Swift's most recent novel, *The Light of Day*, published and long-listed for the Booker Prize: set in south London, where Swift continues to live and write (near Wandsworth Common).

Abbreviations

EA	*Ever After* (paperback edn.; London: Picador,1992)
LD	*The Light of Day* (London: Hamish Hamilton, 2003)
LO	*Last Orders* (London: Picador, 1996)
LS	*Learning to Swim and Other Stories*, ed. Richard Hoyes (Cambridge: Cambridge University Press, 1995)
OTW	*Out of This World* (paperback edn.; Harmondsworth: Penguin Books, 1988)
S.	*Shuttlecock* (paperback edn.; Harmondsworth: Penguin Books, 1982)
SSO	*The Sweet Shop Owner* (paperback edn.; Harmondsworth: Penguin Books, 1983)
W.	*Waterland* (rev. paperback edn.; London: Picador, 1992)

Introduction

Graham Swift is among the very foremost of contemporary British novelists. Since 1980 he has published a volume of short stories and seven novels, the great majority having been highly acclaimed by reviewers and critics and widely read by students and the general public alike (they are translated into over twenty languages). Two – *Waterland* and *Last Orders* – have also been made into films. Among other prestigious international prizes Swift's fiction has been awarded, *Waterland* – which rapidly established itself as a modern classic – received the *Guardian* Fiction Award, the Winifred Holtby Memorial Prize, the Italian Premio Grinzane Cavour, and was short-listed for the Booker Prize in 1983; *Last Orders* won the Booker in 1996; and Swift's most recent novel, *The Light of Day* (2003), was again included in the long short-list for that coveted prize. It is surprising, therefore, that while two or three of Swift's texts have received extended critical analysis, the overall character and development of his novel-writing career has, by contrast, been largely unexamined.

In a *Guardian* 'Profile' on 1 March 2003, immediately after the publication of *The Light of Day*, Swift is quoted as saying:

> There isn't a great deal in my life that you can take and make a hook out of.[...] Why did I become a writer? I can't really come up with any antecedent for it. I'm certainly not from the classic unhappy childhood. I was a student and then I knocked around a bit and then I knuckled down to the job of writing and eventually got published and here I am at novel number whatever it is. There is not much more to it.[1]

Furthermore, back in 1988, Swift is on the record as saying: 'I don't believe in the autobiographical mode of writing', reiterating this position in 1992: 'None of my characters is me, I don't

1

go around looking for material from my life to make a novel. Nor do I turn people I know into characters. Writing in the first person is a complete act of imagination'.[2] Others who know him well (his long-term partner, Candice Rodd, for example, in the same *Guardian* 'Profile' above) also confirm that he does not do much 'real-life' research before beginning a novel but 'imagines and surmises'.[3] While it would be a mistake, therefore, to try and make strong connections between Swift's fiction and his life, some brief biographical details may nevertheless help set the scene for a corpus of work that resonates with repeated locales, characters, relationships, events, themes and tropes.

Graham Swift was born on 4 May 1949 in South London, on the borders of Sydenham and Catford – hence not far from Lewisham and Greenwich (*Waterland*), Bermondsey (*Last Orders*) and Chislehurst (*The Light of Day*); other south London areas that feature centrally are Clapham and Wimbledon Commons in *Shuttlecock* and Wimbledon again in *The Light of Day*. His mother came from the more up-market end of Sydenham, while his father – a naval fighter pilot in the Second World War – was brought up in the lower-class area of Sydenham down the hill. Swift grew up in the 1950s sharply aware of his father's wartime experience and surrounded by 'all the physical evidence of war': 'So the second world war, which I never went through, has been my great history lesson'.[4] That final phrase inescapably invokes the central narrative trope in *Waterland*; and, as we shall see, what one of his fellow students at Cambridge has called 'a real preoccupation with the second world war'[5] became an iterative theme in all but his latest novel.

Educated in south London schools in the 1960s – during which period he had already decided to become a writer – Swift went up to Queens' College, Cambridge, in 1967, where his first short story was published in a college journal and whence he graduated with a First in English in 1970. From 1970 to 1973, while ostensibly undertaking a Ph.D. at the University of York on 'The Role of the City in Nineteenth-Century English Literature', Swift was really devoting all his time to teaching himself to write. 'Having reached the end of my student years,' he later recalled, 'the last three spent posing as a Ph.D. candidate while I secretly began my apprenticeship as a writer', he upped sticks in 1974 and went to Greece for a memorable

2

year teaching English in Volos and writing his first, 'irredeemably awful', novel.[6] On his return to London, he supported himself mainly by part-time teaching in Further Education colleges, which gave him time to write each day. During the later 1970s and early 1980s, Swift began to publish short stories in collections (including *Firebird*, a Penguin anthology of contemporary writing (1982)) and in literary journals (*Punch*, *Stand Magazine* and the *London Magazine*). These stories comprise the volume, *Learning to Swim and Other Stories*, first published by London Magazine Editions in 1982. However, two years earlier, Swift had had his first novel, *The Sweet Shop Owner* (1980), published to largely favourable reviews, while a second, *Shuttlecock*, appeared in 1981, and a third, *Waterland*, was well underway. It was the rapturous reception of the latter in 1983, however – together with Swift's inclusion that year in the Granta *Best of Young British Novelists* collection – that really made his name and allowed him, as he had always hoped, to become a full-time writer. A perfectionist dedicated to and engrossed in his writing, Swift still lives in south London, near Wandsworth Common, and continues to write about it. 'There is', as he himself says, 'not much more to it' than that.

All Graham Swift's fiction, then – apart from his most recent novel – was published, if not written, between 1980 and 1996: in other words, it all 'belongs' in some sense to the late-twentieth-century Britain of Tory Governments – principally those of Mrs Thatcher and then of John Major. *The Light of Day*, on the other hand, is the product of Britain under 'New Labour', but one may well question whether Swift's vision of the broader social and cultural tendencies of his period have altered significantly in this new context – indeed, it may even have become bleaker and more disenchanted. While space constraints preclude analysis of the short stories, the reading of each of Swift's novels that follows here will attempt to identify in them those elements that are symptomatic of late, and then early new, millennial Britain. For the most part narrated by first-person male characters, all the fiction (including the stories collected in *Learning to Swim*) is characterized by a focus on interpersonal, usually fraught, relationships between lovers, husbands and wives, parents and children (when the latter survive the startlingly high incidence of abortion or miscarriage); and on such iterative themes as the interpenetration of past and present, the blurring of distinctions between 'history' and 'story', fact and fiction, 'the real thing' and its substitutes, the possibilities (or not) of redemption in a contemporary social and emotional wasteland. The period within which the stories and novels are primarily located is that of 'the present' (that is, of the time in which they are written), and their setting – implied rather than foregrounded – tends to be urban, middle-class, claustrophobic and loveless. One might add, as I hope to show, that, because the narrative voice is so predominantly male ('history' is very much '*his* story'), the representation of women in Swift's fiction is frequently problematic: several are literally *silenced* in and by the text. There are few 'her-stories' here.

But, although each of Swift's fictions is set in the present, the Second World War is a determinate presence in all but *The Light of Day*, with the First World War and other histories behind that. His novels, in other words, depict a world still bearing the scars of its pasts, one in which most certainties have evaporated and which has become an empty and meretricious simulacrum of what human life is capable of – a world, in shorthand, recognizably 'postmodern', where, in the shadow of nuclear holocaust, as a character in *Waterland* puts it, we approach 'the End of History' (*W.* 19). But what the novels also seem to propose is the possibility of salvaging some vestiges of humanity from postmodern anomie by way of 'telling stories' and of 'love', the former itself an equivocal substitute for the discredited 'grand narrative' of 'History', the latter a conspicuous if problematic theme in contemporary British fiction (symptomatized, perhaps, by the wry title of Doris Lessing's novel, *Love, Again* (1996) – with that weary comma at its centre). This 'new humanism', if such I may call it, is embattled, tentative, provisional and uncertain, as Swift is only too well aware, and his fiction – usually consciously, but on occasions apparently unconsciously, as we shall see – reveals problems with this challenge to postmodern carelessness and emotional atrophy.

While the informing themes and vision of Swift's fiction may be recognizably aligned with postmodern tendencies, is it nevertheless correct to describe him as a 'postmodernist' novelist in terms of his literary affiliations and formal strategies?

4

The answer is at best equivocal. In *The Politics of Postmodernism*, Linda Hutcheon proposes that postmodernist fiction is 'where documentary historical actuality [or 'realist representation'] meets formalist self-reflexivity and parody', and that in 'the paradoxical postmodern form I [...] call "historiographic metafiction"', 'Narrative representation – fictive and historical – comes under [...] subversive scrutiny [...] by having its historical and socio-political grounding sit uneasily alongside its self-reflexivity'.[7] And Swift's *Waterland* is one of the key examples Hutcheon gives of 'historiographic metafiction'[8] (we will see how well it fits her description in the chapter devoted to it). It is a term also entirely appropriate to his next – albeit very different – novel, *Out of This World*, whose central motif for the problematics of 'realist representation' is photography, and to *Ever After*, with its interpolated (purportedly 'real') journal by a Victorian forebear of the narrator's charting his loss of faith during the evolution controversy. While *Last Orders* and *The Light of Day* are less clearly examples of 'historiographic metafiction', they nevertheless continue self-reflexively to problematize the way 'the truth' about 'what really happened' gets told. Furthermore, the narrative structure of Swift's fiction – intercutting 'histories' from the past with the story of the present in a comprehensively disturbed chronology – is at once a critical controversion of the linear realist narrative and a sophisticated display of postmodernist self-consciousness.

In these respects, Swift's work appears properly to be regarded as postmodernist, but not of the extreme kind that abjures all narrative coherence (as we shall see, the underlying chronology of the novels is extraordinarily exact and precisely traceable), or which disconnects itself from history and the world. James Green has recently written that, unlike the compulsively self-conscious postmodern fiction of the 1960s and '70s in America, 'British fiction of the 1980s and '90s expresses a deep conviction about the continuing moral and emotional functions of narrative.[...] The sheer popularity of historiographic metafiction certainly attests to a serious concern with history in contemporary culture'.[9] Such fiction, then, may be seen to represent a positive recognition that narrative drive and historical and social engagement are what both the contemporary novelist and the contemporary reader still believe to be the essential characteristics of 'telling stories'. And there is no doubt that Swift is best located amongst those modern British novelists (*inter alia*, John Fowles, Salman Rushdie, Peter Ackroyd, Antonia Byatt, Julian Barnes) who combine, in what Hutcheon calls 'a complicitous critique',[10] a strong sense of the realist tradition (especially of the nineteenth century – Dickens is manifestly an influence on Swift) with self-reflexive tropes and strategies derived from postmodernism. Such novelists counter-point the inescapable pull of historical understanding with historiographical scepticism about ever being able to tell 'the whole truth' or 'the whole story' (recurrent phrases in Swift's fiction), and feel compelled to confront what Christopher Isherwood once called 'the fantastic realities of the everyday world'[11] while recognizing the impossibility of fully or accurately representing them. Swift's novels, like those of his contemporaries, are – to borrow a phrase from his most recent one – 'reports from the world' (*LD* 138), reports on the way we live now. But such 'reports' are credible only because they themselves know and reveal that any report – fictional or factual – must be partial: it is pertinent here to note that another word for 'report', in the media at least, is 'story'.

Considering Swift's status and reputation, his work as a whole has not received the degree or quality of critical attention one might have expected. While reviews of individual novels have generally been perceptive and positive (except, principally, those of *Out of This World*), academic criticism is patchy (largely on *Waterland* and *Last Orders*) and leaves a lot to be desired. However, in preparing to write this book, I strategically decided not to read any criticism of any of the novels until after I had finished a more or less complete draft. This was for two main reasons: first, it would allow me to work my way independently through Swift's whole *œuvre* in order to produce a comprehensive reading of the fiction uninfluenced by what others had already said; and, secondly, it would preclude clogging up an introductory guide with references to diverse critical works or arcane critical debates. It is for the reader to judge whether this strategy has worked or not, but for the writer it turned out to be invaluable.

Given the complexity and disturbance – but also the precision

– of the narrative chronologies in Swift's fiction, together with his acutely self-conscious use of language, the critical methodology I have elected to use here in my novel-by-novel readings is an old and tested praxis under a new name: what I choose to call 'descriptive interpretation'. This is, in effect, a form of close textual reading that at once lays out the trajectory of the work before the reader and highlights the interconnections, resonances and thematic patterns that may then be better descried in the rich and dense textuality of the novel itself. Another way of putting it would be to say that such a critical method 'presses' the text – in both senses of the word press: 'to bear heavily upon' and 'to urge, encourage, entreat' – to 'speak for itself'. Hence the reader will find here extensive short quotation, often from right across the novel's breadth, which is intended to ground very firmly in its textuality the evidence for what I believe the novel is conveying. The danger here, of course, is that the novel so dissected will in effect be refashioned as a work that I have now 'rewritten' by reading it so closely through my own pair of spectacles. But if criticism is to abjure this concentration on the textuality of the text, then it might just as well hang up those spectacles and find something better to do. With a sophisticated and perspicacious contemporary novelist like Graham Swift, however – one whose fiction is a self-reflexive historiographical anatomy of our own society and culture – such an abdication of the critical function, right or wrong, would seem to be perverse: an irresponsible and ignorant rebuff to Swift's attempt to offer 'telling stories' for our enlightenment.

1

Early Novels: *The Sweet Shop Owner* and *Shuttlecock*

It is perhaps too temptingly easy to regard a writer's early productions through the lens of the later work that you have read first: in Graham Swift's case, reading back from *Waterland*, say, may be to cast his earlier fiction in the mould of that much admired third novel. On the other hand, it is often illuminating to see from the beginning how consistent (or not) are an author's cast of mind, fictional strategies and preferred subject matter as they work towards fuller realization in the well-known books of their maturity, and Swift's first novels are no exception. Indeed, from the start, recurrent characteristics of his writing are inescapably evident: first-person narration by male characters (an exception is *The Sweet Shop Owner* – and even there the third person is used equivocally); a focus on damaged personal relationships in a contemporary bourgeois setting; and early forays into themes that have since become Swift's trademark: the interpenetration of past and present, what is 'real' and what is not, the problematics of 'telling stories'.

The Sweet Shop Owner recounts the lives of Willy Chapman, his wife, Irene, their daughter Dorothy, and the relationships between the three of them, from 1937 when Willy and Irene first meet and marry, through the death of Irene in July/August of 1973, to 'the present' of the novel, a June day in 1974 that is also Dorothy's twenty-fifth birthday. During this day, Willy secretly pays off the staff of his sweet shop, and then waits willingly, on the final page of the book, for the heart attack that will finally kill him. The novel thus spans the Second World War, but also looks back to events and their effects from the First World War onwards. Two points may be deduced from this summary: first, that ordinary lives – and they are very ordinary – are somehow contextualized by the twentieth century's major wars; and, second, that the chronology of the novel is extremely precise, right down to exact months and years.

Let me take the second point first, and return to the significance of war later on. One might reasonably ask: what is so extraordinary about chronological precision? have we not come to expect it in the linear narratives of conventional realist fiction? But *The Sweet Shop Owner* is not a conventional linear narrative: rather, it is the first full-length example of Swift using a disturbed chronology that cuts backwards and forwards between the present and its various pasts. The novel is in three parts of more or less equal length (Part I, pre-war period and Second World War ; Part II, post-war years up to *c*.1965; Part III, later 1960s and early 1970s), but it is further divided into thirty-nine numbered short chapters that offer fragments of the period 1937–74 in dislocated order (sometimes shifting from one period to another even in the same section). Only by careful textual detective work, therefore, is it possible to date the various sections, and what *is* extraordinary then is to discover how precise the underlying chronology actually is. For example, we are never told explicitly that 'the present' is in 1974, nor in the opening section of the novel that this is indeed 'the present', although we fairly quickly learn that it is a hot, and somehow momentous, day in June (*SSO* 10). However, during a conversation with his shop assistant, Willy says: 'I last had a holiday [...] in sixty-three' (*SSO* 33), and a couple of pages later, Mrs Cooper replies: ' "Sixty-three, Mr Chapman? That's eleven years ago." "Yes. Eleven years" ' (*SSO* 35). Furthermore, on the third page of the novel, as on the final one (*SSO* 11, 233), Willy, mentally addressing the absent Dorothy, muses: 'today [...] is your birthday'; as we know that she was born in June 1949 (*SSO* 10), and was 20 in 1969 (*SSO* 161), we can once more confirm that this 'present' day is in June 1974. A similar process of deduction from hints spread throughout the narrative is possible for other key events or moments, and underlines the importance for Swift of having a very exact foundational chronology that he then strategically fragments and disperses. Why might he do this?

As we shall also see in all Swift's later novels, the principal reason is at once to show how the past is a determinate presence in the present (especially in the consciousness of the narrators), and to 'explain' (a recurrent Swift word) how the present has come to be as it is. By counterpointing fragments from different periods, he is able to build up in the reader's mind a chronological mosaic that gradually forms itself into a discernible pattern of the interlocking moments – both personal and historical – that fashion a person's life in the present. One is tempted to call it 'the whole story', but that is another phrase that frequently appears in Swift's fiction, and it is always a problematic one. So, as we read the opening pages of *The Sweet Shop Owner*, we begin to want to know: what has happened to cause Willy Chapman to send his clearly estranged daughter Dorothy £15,000 of her dead mother's money (*SSO* 9); whether Dorothy knew 'where that money really came from' (*SSO* 11); and why Willy prepares himself so carefully to go to his shop for 'the last time' (*SSO* 12). In effect, the rest of the novel is an explanation of this 'present' day.

The dominant narrative mode of the novel is in the third person, and, apart from the short story 'Learning to Swim', is the only example of Swift's fiction narrated in this fashion. But, even so, the third-person narrative of both story and novel is not of the clear-cut 'omniscient' kind; rather, it is closer to what narratologists now call 'focalization' (an earlier term for it was 'point-of-view'). This is when a third-person narrative nevertheless tells the story from what can only be the perspective of a character or consciousness (a 'focalizer') within the story. In *The Sweet Shop Owner* it is mainly located in Willy's consciousness ('So he had seen her perhaps for the last time. [. . .] But she would come, surely. Now she had the money. She would come – she hadn't said she *wouldn't*' (*SSO* 9)), but is also interspersed with passages where he is mentally addressing Dorothy in a mixture of the first and second person ('Do you first remember those moments, Dorry, in the early hours? Sometimes I'd pick you up and walk you round the room' (*SSO* 115)). In addition, there is Irene's first-person account of her life before she knew Willy in chapter 7, apparently addressed to him as he rests with his head in her lap (' "How little you know me, Willy. How little you know of that young girl" ' (*SSO* 49)), but which the novel

10

later implies he never heard (*SSO* 150). While these forms of narrative are obviously a way of accessing the mindset of the main characters, their principal point, in combination with the fragmented chronology described above, is to reveal how the present is a product of the past and what that past comprises. The central issue here is the nature of the relationship between Willy and Irene, and the question of why Willy became a sweet shop owner.

It transpires in Irene's silent first-person 'soliloquy' that her beauty as a girl was fetishized by her family, but leads to a young man raping her on the way back from a drive (*SSO* 52). She suffers a breakdown and is institutionalized in a 'Home' (as are so many of Swift's later characters also). In order to escape her family after recovering from this, Irene calculatedly marries Willy in 1937, and with money given by her mother (who herself inherited it only because her three brothers were all killed in the First World War – a point to be returned to), buys Willy a sweet shop, thus laying down the basis of their future together. Willy muses:

> And what she really meant [...] was: I will buy you a shop [...] I will install you in it and see that you have all you need. Then I'll watch. [...] That will content me. [...] I shan't interfere, only watch. You will be free, absolved; for the responsibility – don't you see – will be mine. [...] And all I ask in return for this is that there be no question of love. (*SSO* 21–2)

The nub of Swift's novel lies in that last line: for although Willy loves Irene profoundly, he is never allowed to express it: 'If the word love is never spoken, does it mean there isn't any love?' (*SSO* 116). Even as Irene goes into labour with Dorothy, Willy can think only of 'the words he was forbidden to speak ['I love you'], which broke the terms of the bargain' (*SSO* 102). A further aspect of this bargain of denial is Willy's recognition that, in becoming pregnant, Irene was 'labouring to pay a debt' (*SSO* 101): 'she had given him, in her place, Dorothy' (*SSO* 127). Not surprisingly, there is no love lost between mother and daughter, and, although Willy idolizes Dorothy, she gradually alienates herself from him, too. Having received the £15,000 of her mother's money that she has demanded of him, she writes him the short, cold letter with which the novel opens (*SSO* 9). This is a world emptied of love, and Willy, potentially so capable of it, is

shown to become no more than a simulacrum of a 'real' person –
even of a sweet shop owner: a hollow man who would 'adopt a
shop-keeper's manner. And in time it would be wholly
plausible' (*SSO* 42). On his last day, he announces what is in
effect his epitaph: 'I never believed you could have *the real thing*'
(*SSO* 184; emphasis added) – a phrase that resonates throughout
this novel and recurs in all those that follow.

For what the 'bargain' with Irene 'really means' is that Willy
'would play his part.... What was easier?' (*SSO* 44), that he sees
his whole life and career thereafter as no more than a
'performance' (*SSO* 133, 196–7) and himself as 'a performer'
(*SSO* 58) or 'some cut-out figure' (*SSO* 132). Such forms of
acting, of putting up a false front, again become an iterative
trope in much of Swift's fiction, and are the converse of that
illusive grail, 'the real thing'. Willy regards the contents of his
shop as equally deceptive: his window display was 'something
which promised real goods, real riches within, but was itself
quite specious' (*SSO* 131). Indeed, the shop – with its relentless
increase over the years in sales and turnover – seems to mirror
the growing prosperity of the 1950s and 1960s in British society
at large, which the novel also sketches in contextually as the
years pass, the implication being that the affluent society, like
the sweet shop itself, is 'specious': all material surface and no
spiritual substance, promising 'the real thing' but no more than
a simulacrum. As Willy prepares to close his shop for the last
time and gets ready to die, he looks round valedictorially at 'the
plastic dolls, action-men and model knights in armour, whose
promise was to be like the real thing' (*SSO* 213).

In order to explain why the world the novel depicts is so
superficial and emotionally atrophied, it is necessary to return
to the presence of war as an iterative motif: as the history
behind the novel's story. The chronological story begins in the
years immediately preceding the Second World War; covers the
war years when the sweet shop is closed for business (the nation
now being involved in 'the real thing' (*SSO* 57)); mentions the
imminence of war during the Cuban crisis in 1962 (*SSO* 140);
and reprints the newspaper headline 'PEACE BID FAILS' in the
present of 1974 on two occasions (*SSO* 17, 39). But what is more
pointed is the continual association of Irene with war. Further
textual detective work (we can deduce she was 50 in 1964 (*SSO*

120)) reveals that Irene was born in 1914, the year the First World War began, thus making her the first of a significant number of Swift's 'war-babies' or 'children of war'. On their honeymoon in 1937, and again in 1938, Irene, reading the newspapers, and like some prophetess of doom, suddenly announces: 'There will be a war, Willy' (SSO 31, 56). Both she and Willy, neither combatants in 'the real thing', keep records – in her case of the numbers of ration books issued, in his of helmets and packs to the troops who pass through the quartermaster's stores, the novel commenting: 'History was drawing up its inventory' (SSO 79). Both Irene's brothers join up and see action ('the real thing at last' (SSO 75)), with one of them lost at sea. Despite Willy saying to Dorothy, 'I think what she wants is peace' (SSO 142 – 'PEACE BID FAILS' is given an ironic twist in this context), it is as though Irene is somehow complicit with war, is so intimate with it that it is like her second nature: 'No, it wasn't war, destruction that she feared. It almost protected her, that great ominous blackness, as if she knew where she stood with it' (SSO 60). Perhaps most tellingly, all three of Irene's uncles were killed in the First World War, this being the reason why her mother, and then Irene in her turn, inherit the money the brothers would otherwise have had (SSO 82). This is what Irene uses to buy the sweet shop, and it is also the money Willy hands on to Dorothy just before his death in 1974, silently asking her: 'Do you know where that money really came from?' (SSO 11). Right at the end of the novel, as he waits to die, Willy again muses to Dorothy: 'That money was always meant to be passed on. It was never [Irene's]; it was only a token of something.[...] It never belonged to her. It belonged to the bronze soldiers [Irene's uncles]' (SSO 221–2). What was it 'a token of'? A little earlier it has been described as 'only converted history', which will 'encumber' Dorothy (SSO 217), the inference surely being that this is a kind of blood money, 'a token' of the destructive effect the First World War has had in fashioning the rest of the twentieth century, including its compounding by the Second World War. And Irene, born in 1914, desperate for peace but indelibly tainted by war, becomes the figuration of the cost paid by humankind for those wars. The refusal of love, the destruction of it in others, the creation of a meretricious simulacrum of a life (Willy, the sweet shop), the perverse rejection of 'the real thing', all symbolize the way the later twentieth century is the offspring of its violent parents.

The matrix of the past shaping the features of the present in *The Sweet Shop Owner* represents Swift's early attempt to engage with the notion of 'history', a theme that will receive much fuller and more sophisticated treatment in later novels. This is flagged in Irene's narrative when she says that the survivors of the First World War 'wanted to forget history. They wanted new life.' (*SSO* 50) Paradoxically, the kind of 'new' death-in-life that Irene constructs with Willy ('Nothing must be touched, nothing must be changed' (*SSO* 55)) is an attempt to 'forget history' and to live outside it: during the blackout in the Second World War, she thinks: 'we do not belong to history' (*SSO* 60). With the VE Day celebrations taking place as the war ends ('"Three cheers for Victory!" Victory! Victory! echoed the cry. But no one used the other word that had hissed gently in the falling rain: Peace' (*SSO* 85)), the novel's use of the word 'history' becomes more ironic: 'Soon history would be honoured' (*SSO* 83), but only by bronze memorials proclaiming 'Undying memories' (*SSO* 86), themselves simulacra of 'the real thing'. In the immediately post-war world, the shops in the high street reopen, 'as if history could be circumvented and the war (what war?) veiled by the allurements of their windows' (*SSO* 98): Willy's own shop displays cinema advertisements for 'John Mills and Kenneth More in cheerful re-enactments of the war. History enshrined in make-believe.[...] What war? A packet of gum please, and another card in the series "Great Battles of World War Two"' (*SSO* 131).

What the novel seems to be suggesting is that, while the reality of war is forgotten or obscured by 'history' and 'make-believe', its presence is nevertheless determinate in the post-war world. It is no coincidence that, in his final musings to Dorothy, Willy asks: 'And have you escaped history [...] Found new life? Encumbered with all those things of hers, encumbered with the money I sent you (that money, which was only converted history)' (*SSO* 216–17). For Willy, only a visit from Dorothy on that present day in June 1974 'can dissolve history now' (*SSO* 217) – a visit, in other words, that would represent love and controvert the loveless legacy of war. Needless to say, Dorothy does not come, and Willy, about to die, sums things up: 'You might have had the real thing. You got the money.[...] And what will you buy with it, Dorry? History?' (*SSO* 221–2). History represents the illusion of progress that obscures the two 'real' casualties of war: peace and love. And in the profoundly damaged but deceptive and self-deceived consumerist world of Swift's late twentieth century, 'BIDS' for both those 'real things' seem to have 'FAILED'.

Shuttlecock is the first of Swift's novels to deploy a single first-person male narrator, Prentis – although within his narrative long passages are reproduced, as though verbatim, from his father's Second World War memoir, entitled *Shuttlecock: The Story of a Secret Agent* (he served with the French Resistance, was captured by the Germans, tortured and escaped – or did he?). Prentis reveals himself to be a thoroughly unpleasant man – especially as husband and father – although he undergoes something of a transformation as the novel unfolds. Deeply insecure from living in his hero father's shadow, he is a petty tyrant at home who tries to browbeat his own two sons by banishing the TV set that the boys watch all the time. Indeed, the television becomes a kind of symbol for the dehumanized domestic universe of the Prentis family – and, by extension, the wider contemporary society: 'My own sons don't look up to their father. They look up to the Bionic Man.[...] The Bionic Man performs impossible feats, solves impossible riddles and bears no relation to anything natural. But they look up to him, not their father' (*S.* 9–10) ('natural/unnatural' is a binary that permeates the book). But it is Prentis's sexual relationship with his wife, Marian, that principally 'bears no relation to anything natural'. Bolstered by 'paraphernalia' from sex shops, Prentis is 'systematically and cold-bloodedly, like a torturer bent on breaking his victim [...] turning my wife into a whore' (*S.* 75). Believing that 'sexual adventure is the only form of adventure left to us in our age' (*S.* 74), his nightly 'sexual experiments with Marian' are carried out ultimately 'to receive enlightenment' (*S.* 73). That Prentis is still in outer darkness, and likely to remain there by seeking enlightenment through 'the most elaborate *charades*, the most strenuous *performances*' (*S.* 73; emphases added – we are not in the presence of 'the real thing' here) cannot be in doubt, but the search for 'enlightenment' is nevertheless a central, if problematic, theme of the novel.

Prentis works in a police subdepartment that deals with the

records of 'dead crimes' (*S.* 15): those that were committed long ago or are officially closed: 'We sit in a strong-room of secrets.[...] For many of our files are sealed. Only Quinn can unseal and reseal them' (*S.* 16). Quinn is Prentis's boss, a curious mixture of Big Brother from *1984* and Wemmick from *Great Expectations*, whom Prentis both fears and envies, and who will turn out to be central in *Shuttlecock*'s concern with 'unsealing secrets' – a theme that will also resurface throughout Swift's later novels. Significantly, the office is half underground with no windows, and is referred to by Prentis as 'this dungeon' (*S.* 17), and an emphasis on the subterranean recurs throughout the novel. On an 'Underground train', people behave 'with suspicion and menace. It's as if everybody is trying to search out everybody else's secret, and the assumption is that this secret will always be a weakness' (*S.* 25); 'Z', a man involved in one of the 'dead crimes', and later connected with the mystery surrounding Prentis's father, 'committed suicide (by stepping in front of an Underground train)' (*S.* 29); during the Second World War, Prentis's father, a secret agent working with the French Resistance ('the Underground'), is held captive in the 'dungeons' of Château Martine, the Gestapo headquarters near the village of Combe-les-Dames (*S.* 143). Much of the setting here, then – to borrow the title of Swift's latest novel – is out of 'the light of day'.

The novel is ostensibly an account – which Prentis is significantly writing down (*S.* 39 – hence his account 'becomes' the novel) – of a short period of his life in the late spring of 'the present' (*c.*1980). We hear about the missing files assumed to have been removed by Quinn (whose job Prentis covets: 'to be in a position to *know* [...] no longer to be in the dark' (*S.* 71), and about his visits to his father, now in a mental institution and completely silent after a breakdown two years before (confined silent figures are a recurrent feature of Swift's fiction). As a consequence of this silence ('there is [...] so much to be explained' (*S.* 43)), he is rereading his father's war memoir, *Shuttlecock: The Story of a Secret Agent*, in order 'to know the whole truth', especially about 'what was going on inside' Prentis senior: 'What was it like, what was it really like?' (*S.* 52). Here we have an early instance of a phrase that will haunt all Swift's fiction: 'the whole truth' (sometimes reinflected as 'the whole story'). The problem for Prentis, however, is that when Dad describes his feelings, 'he conveys them [...] as in some made-up adventure story; so that sometimes this book which is all fact seems to me like fiction, like something that never really took place. What really happened, Dad, at [...] Combe-les-Dames?' (S. 52). That other recurrent question, 'what really happened', is now combined in a tentatively self-reflexive way with the blurring of distinctions between 'fact' and 'fiction' (and, by implication, 'story' and 'history'), hence announcing what will become a central issue in the next novel, Waterland, if not in all the later fiction.

'What really happened?' becomes the central question about Prentis senior's wartime exploits, his written account of them, and the partial revelation by Quinn to Prentis of a 'dead case' about 'X', 'Y' and 'Z' involving the latter's father that seems to have culminated in his breakdown and silence. Basically, the question is: was Prentis senior a war hero who spied on German targets for the Resistance, was captured and tortured by the Gestapo, but heroically escaped from them (as his book implies); or was he 'a coward and a traitor' (S. 183) who broke under interrogation, thus betraying several Resistance units and ensuring the exposure of three fellow British agents, and who was then 'allowed [...] to escape' (S. 183) by the Germans in return? And apropos of his book: are 'the gaps, the hazy areas' (S. 105) in the two chapters about his imprisonment in Château Martine the result of 'something so terrible that it cannot be repeated, cannot be spoken or written of', an 'experience beyond words' (S. 106), or deliberate obfuscations to hide the fact of 'what really happened'? Significantly, Prentis nevertheless finds these chapters 'more vivid, more real, more believable than any other part of the book' – despite the fact that 'Dad's writing style becomes [...] more imaginative, more literary, more speculative' (S. 106–7). Is this fact or is it fiction – and which is 'more real, more believable'? Equally, is the father's two-year-old silence the result of experiences so awful that they have led to 'gaping holes in the memory' (S. 105), or is it 'the perfect defence: impenetrable silence' (S. 184)? Is his book true or false when he writes: 'there is much about my days at the Château which I simply do not remember.[...] perhaps the truth is that certain things defy retelling' (S. 139). Does the final sentence here imply volition or blind impulse, and can 'the truth' be silence? As Prentis begins the attempt 'to know what's true and what isn't' (S. 85) by 'delving into untold privacies [...] the darker byways of other people's lives' (S. 98), Quinn asks him 'the simple question: Is it better to know things or not to know them? Wouldn't we sometimes be happier not knowing them?' (S. 118 – again a dilemma repeated throughout Swift's novels). Chapter 32, in which Prentis visits Quinn at home, is a key moment in the novel. The buttoned-up dictator of the office here transforms, Wemmick-like (he, too, is a custodian of the secrets of 'Little Britain' in *Great Expectations*), into a benign human being in his domestic retreat. Here, Quinn again wonders: 'how much you should tell, and how much you should keep silent, and how much should you know' (S. 176), and it becomes clear that he has been destroying files in order to spare living relatives 'needless painful knowledge' about the subjects of 'that great heap of secrets at the office' (S. 176). He sums up by saying: ' – the best, the securest position to be in is not to know. But once you do know, you can't do anything about it. You can't get rid of knowledge' (S. 177), a little later adding: 'It's hard enough withholding the truth when you're sure it's the truth you're withholding. But it's ten times worse when there's even the shadow of a doubt that it might not be the truth at all' (S. 182).

Gradually, Quinn reveals that 'File E' of the X, Y and Z case involves Prentis's father, containing letters from the now dead X that were intended to blackmail him by claiming that Prentis senior, rather than being a war hero, had cracked under interrogation and had in fact been a traitor. At this moment, Prentis junior experiences 'this strange feeling of release. *I* had escaped; I was free' (S. 183), the significance of which will become clear later. It transpires that X's letters were composed 'about two years ago' – in other words, 'when Dad had his breakdown' (S. 184). When Prentis claims that the last chapters of his father's book are 'too convincing not to be real' (S. 186), Quinn makes the case against Prentis senior by arguing that if 'his hero's reputation rested ultimately upon a lie', then 'the *true* exploits [...] can be treated almost like fiction, but the part of the book that's really a lie – that's where all the urgency is' (S. 187). On Prentis senior's state of mind as he is confined in the

Château's dungeons and undergoing torture, Quinn now speculates: 'it's a mystery; I don't know *what really happened*. But you can be sure of one thing. If he did betray, he only did what any ordinary, *natural* human being would have done – he saved his own skin' (*S*. 190; emphases added). He then reveals that in File E, there is also a letter from X to Z alleging that Prentis senior had been having an affair with Z's wife for nearly a year before Z committed suicide, and that X's letter to 'Dad' also threatened to make this public. Prentis is by now convinced that his father was a traitor and that his breakdown into silence clinches it, but Quinn equivocates once more: 'It doesn't clinch the *truth* of anything [....] A breakdown can be triggered by a false accusation [...] as well as by the real thing' (*S*. 197; earlier, apropos of 'the wife's *story*' in the Z case (*S*. 87; emphasis in original), Quinn asks: 'What's true, Prentis, tell me: what really happens or what people will accept as true?' (*S*. 89)). But what is 'the real thing', and which 'story' is true or false? Quinn proposes destroying File E, before which, however, he gives Prentis the option of reading it in order to ascertain whether the allegations were indeed true or false: 'then suddenly I knew I wanted to be uncertain, I wanted to be *in the dark*' (*S*. 199; emphasis added). The file is burnt; he will never – could he ever? – know 'the whole truth' about 'what really happened' – and nor will we.

Before Prentis leaves, Quinn tells him he is retiring and that Prentis will be promoted to his job, and on his way home Prentis feels as though he has 'emerged out of some confinement' (*S*. 203). The last three chapters of the novel take place six months after Quinn has left the office, where Prentis is carrying on the protective work of removing files that contain 'needless painful knowledge' (*S*. 176): 'All these little bits of poisoned paper I am slowly dropping into oblivion. What people don't know can't hurt them ...' (*S*. 212; it is now clear that he has indeed been Quinn's 'a-Prentis'). He has ceased to be a tyrant at home, calling this his 'transformation' (*S*. 209), and he stops reading 'Dad's book. I inquired no further' (*S*. 214). The final chapter opens: 'And today –' (*S*. 215), so we know we are right in the present; and what 'today' holds is a family outing to Camber Sands. Prentis remembers that what attracted him about Camber when he was a boy were 'the relics of the war that

19

still littered the region.[...] All this was scenery from that awesome drama in which Dad had only recently been an actor' (that final word by now contains a telling irony), and he recalls having 'a vision of the war as a simple, romantic affair' (*S.* 216). When the family arrive, the younger son Peter asks: ' "What are those rusty metal things over there, Dad?" Dad: "Oh, they're something left over from the war".[...] Peter: "Oh." (Unenlightened [...] but just a little bit afraid [...] that the rusty metal things might still be dangerous)' (*S.* 219). We have seen in the course of the novel just how 'unromantic' war is, and how 'relics' of the Second World War still 'litter' the present and remain 'dangerous': Dad, X, Y and Z and their families, Quinn, and, most importantly, Prentis himself. The whole of chapter 27 is only seven lines long – in Swift's fiction, very short chapters regularly foreground highly significant content: 'I was born in August 1945. I must have been conceived when Dad came home, after his escape, from France. Mum and Dad together in the autumn of '44.[...] *I am a product of those times and of all that happened in the Château Martine*' (*S.* 151; emphases added). Like Irene in *The Sweet Shop Owner*, Prentis is a 'child of war', formed in the matrix of that brutalizing and dehumanizing event, in which, amongst many other casualties, was the distinction between fact and fiction: a son always in the shadow of a hero father who may have 'cracked' and thereafter lived a lie. The implication is that Prentis's own inhumanity in the early parts of the novel is the result of the atrophying of love – which is another offspring of war.

But in this early novel (it becomes less perceptible in later ones) redemption seems realizable. Prentis's exorcism of his father's myth and the past it represents releases him, so that he is able to be 'transformed' and rehumanized in other ways too. Right at the end of the book, he and Marian make love in the sand dunes: 'We had to be quick, quick as sparrows', and this reminds him of the 'magical words' his biology teacher had used when showing him and his classmates a hamster many years before: 'a piece of nature' (*S.* 219). With these words, the novel ends. However, if we return to the chapter in which Prentis recounts his sexual experiments with the 'pliant' Marian, we find him musing:

Making love ought to be *the most natural thing*, oughtn't it?[...] I've been watching the sparrows copulating on our guttering.[...] And sometimes that is just how I see it with Marian and me: a little careless, unadorned instant, like the sparrows; a little flutter of wings and hearts: *at one with nature*. Perhaps it was like that once, long ago. For Marian and me. For all of us. But now you have to go through the most elaborate charades, the most strenuous performances to receive enlightenment. (*S.* 73; emphases added)

Central to the point here is the relating of spontaneous sex and 'love' with 'nature'. Prentis's 'book' (and thus the novel, too) begins with a memory of the hamster he loved as a child, but which he also tortures. Significantly, Prentis asks himself the rhetorical question: 'For what else is love [...] than being close to nature?' (*S.* 35), but his world, a product of war – his father noted that what 'most embodies the evil of war, is not [...] its human violence (for humans cause wars), but its wilful disregard for nature' (*S.* 108) – is loveless and contains scarcely 'anything natural' – from sex to the 'underground' office and its secrets to Bionic Man and zoos. The 'untransformed' Prentis is 'very fond of zoos' (*S.* 152), which his son Martin counters by pointing out that animals in zoos are "not the real thing [...] A lion in a cage isn't a real lion"' (*S.* 153–4). Defeated, Prentis pointedly thinks: 'what else can you do these days, *if you want to be close to nature*, but put it in a cage?' (154; emphasis added). Martin – his 'own hero' once free of 'this *synthetic* hero', Bionic Man (*S.* 211; emphasis added) – is as close as anyone gets to accessing 'the real thing', until Marian and Prentis, free of the 'cage' of his father's wartime past, rediscover it copulating like sparrows in the dunes at Camber Sands.

Unless, that is, Prentis senior had experienced it during his escape from Château Martine (note the château's name: Prentis thinks of Martin as 'his grandfather's grandson' (*S.* 84)). At one point in his book, the father writes that 'of all the humiliations and cruelties [...] none, I think, was more demoralizing, more appalling than this nakedness' (*S.* 145), a sentence that causes Prentis junior, in his pursuit of the 'real' heart of the book, to exclaim: 'suddenly, I think I am there' (*S.* 147). Fleeing naked from the Gestapo, his father notes: 'I experienced all the agonies of a hunted animal' (*S.* 164), but a little later, he reflects: 'I was trying to turn myself into an anonymous creature of the woods.[...] If only I could follow their example, disappear into holes and roots. Merge with the forest....' (*S.* 169). Most significant, however, is his comment: 'I have come to believe – a blatant case of the pathetic fallacy, no doubt – that the woods and the trees are always on the side of the fugitive and the victim, never on the side of the oppressor' (*S.* 164). 'The pathetic fallacy' (John Ruskin's phrase for the anthropomorphic attribution of human feelings to the natural world, and now more generally denoting an intimate relationship between human-kind and nature) is referred to again in chapter 34 (at two lines and one word in total the shortest in the book, and therefore, like chapter 27, clearly of central import). After his visit to Quinn, and at home again with Marian '(she is still talking to her plants)', he asks her: 'do you believe in the pathetic fallacy? That it's really a fallacy, I mean?' (*S.* 215). The implied answers must surely be, respectively: 'Yes' and 'No'. By way of his father's extreme experience during the war – whatever it was that 'really happened' no longer bothers him – Prentis has achieved an understanding of the necessary and fundamental bond between human beings and nature, and that this is the source from which love can develop. His 'transformation' and rehumanization, we might suggest, are dependent on under-standing his father's experience of total nakedness and reduc-tion to the most basic animal existence. Whether Graham Swift had in mind King Lear's famous speeches when he meets Edgar as 'Poor Tom' in the storm on the heath in Act III Scene iv of Shakespeare's play is a moot point, but a couple of references to them will not be inappropriate here. Lear first addresses 'Poor naked wretches, wheresoe'er you are', of whom he has hitherto 'ta'en |Too little care', exclaiming: 'Take physic, pomp; | Expose thyself to feel what wretches feel';[1] and then, as his madness/sanity/humanity expands, he confronts the naked Edgar:

> 'Is man no more than this? Consider him well.[...] Ha! here's three on's are sophisticated. Thou art the thing itself; unaccommodated man is no more but such a poor, bare, forked animal as thou art. Off, off, you lendings! Come, unbutton here.
>
> [*Tearing off his clothes.*][2]

What Prentis realizes is that his father, in his extemity, also became 'a poor, bare, forked animal': 'the thing itself' – a phrase that surely also brings to mind that other phrase: 'the real thing'.

What Swift's early novels seem to establish for us, then, are certain iterative and interpenetrating themes and issues: the presence of the past in the present; the impact of the twentieth century's two world wars; the condition of contemporary Britain – partly as a result of those wars; the failure or redemptive potential of love; the confusion of fact and fiction, truth and falsehood, history and story; the elusiveness of 'the real thing' or the 'whole story'; the unsealing of 'secrets' and the impossibility of finally knowing 'what really happened'; the ambivalence of 'telling stories' – all issues that receive highly sophisticated treatment in Swift's next novel, the one many regard as his masterpiece: *Waterland*.

2

Waterland

Where better to start discussing this big, complex, clever novel than with its title, thence proceeding to its two epigraphs? The word 'Waterland' is, of course, Graham Swift's coinage, which, by running the two elements together as one word, suggests the indissoluble intermingling of earth and water, the forming of a kind of compound (where the whole has properties of its own that are not necessarily those of its constituent parts) or hybrid (which again is qualitatively different from the two or more species from which it is derived). The novel makes a great deal of the endless process of claiming and then reclaiming land from the waters in the Fens of eastern England; the building of dykes, canals and drainage systems; the constant endangering of such systems by the water's equally relentless attempts to reclaim the land for itself; and the murkiness, therefore, of the liquid land or earthy water that dominates the habitat of the Fens: 'His eyes encounter a brown and silent fog. Suspended silt. Stirred-up silt. A domain where earth and water mingle' (*W*. 188). But once having read the novel, we may see that the title-word flags other forms of interpenetration (compounds, hybrids) with which *Waterland* centrally concerns itself: past and present, history and story, fact and fiction, the impossibility of separating them out one from the other, and the impenetrability of the swirling, murky discourses that compose and relate them.

Hence, the point of the novel's second epigraph – 'Ours was the marsh country ...' (a quotation from Dickens's *Great Expectations*) – where 'marsh country' is, of course, exactly 'waterland', but which takes on a further resonance by following the first epigraph: a dictionary definition of the original Greek, and then Latin, word *Historia*: '1. inquiry, investigation, learning. 2. a) a narrative of past events, history. b) any kind of narrative:

account, tale, story'. The same word for both 'history' *and* 'story'? – unstable and treacherous terrain, indeed. But both the words 'history' and 'story' do, in fact, derive from the word *historia* – 'learning by inquiry' (it is worth noticing in passing, therefore, that in its origins 'story' means a form of *knowledge*, a *way of knowing*). Our two words come down to us by way of the earlier English usage in which both 'story' and 'history' can be, as Raymond Williams put it, 'an account of either imaginary events or of events supposed to be true'.[1] But where the modern French word *histoire* retains both meanings, from the fifteenth century onwards the English word bifurcates, so that 'history' comes to mean 'an account of past real events', but 'story' includes 'less formal accounts of past events and accounts of imagined events'.[2]

We may expect in the novel *Waterland*, then, a strategic blurring of distinctions between apparently discrete entities – especially past and present, history and story. Formally, this is principally achieved by Swift's use of a disturbed chronology that offers the reader 'histories' of several different past periods interspersed with 'stories' of the present but not in linear order. (Indeed, as the present chapter proceeds, it will be worth registering how far-flung are the page references to quotations from the novel that I have brought together to support my reading.) However, as in *The Sweet Shop Owner*, the underlying chronology is extremely precise, often down to a specific month and day (for example, Thomas Atkinson strikes his wife, Sarah, with the blow from which she never recovers her sanity in January 1820 (*W.* 76); in October 1874, terrible floods engulf the town of Gildsey, and on 25 October there are rumours that Sarah Atkinson's ghost has been seen (*W.* 100–2); Dick Crick kills Freddie Parr during the night of 25–6 July 1943 (*W.* 35). In addition, 'real' historical events are referred to throughout, including the French Revolution, the First and Second World Wars; and, as before, it is perfectly possible to extrapolate from the text a full sequential chronology of all the events, real and made up, that the novel contains.

Let us start with the novel's chronological 'present'. It is set in south-east London in 1980 (but note how far on are the page numbers that establish this: *W.* 127, 129). Tom Crick, a history teacher who is about to lose his job because the school is 'cutting back on history' (*W.* 5), and his wife, Mary, who in 1979 'began this love-affair ... with God' (*W.* 41), are a childless couple living in Greenwich. Their world – only ever lightly sketched in – typifies the comfortable, somewhat vacuous, bourgeois ambience of 'the present' in most of Swift's fiction:

> They acquire regular habits, spiced with unspectacular variations.[...] Holidays: he, true to form, prefers historical associations; *she is incurious.*[...] Not having a family [...] they do not lack for money, indeed are almost embarrassingly comfortable: the 'enviable Greenwich home' (Regency, porticoed front door) [...] They acquire regular habits and regular diversions. So much so that three decades pass as if little has happened, as if without event [...] (*W.* 123; emphasis added – the significance of Mary's 'incuriosity' will become clear later on)

Equally, the postmodern pub where Tom and the schoolboy, Price, have a drink combines the ersatz past and the 'virtual' present in anachronistic counterpoint: 'The Duke's Head. Mock red velvet. Mock Tudor oak, framing mock Georgian coach-lamps. Amidst the period anomalies, electronic growls, TV-game bleepings. How we advance ...' (*W.* 258). And a Safeways supermarket in Lewisham is described in ironic consumerist detail:

> All the couples with cars to load are eager to be home. They've got all the good things that supermarkets provide. They've got their canned soups and frozen meat, their breakfast cereals and scrubbed vegetables in polythene bags; they've got their cat food, dog food, washing powder, paper tissues, cling film and aluminium foil. But there's something someone hasn't got. (*W.* 155)

The 'something someone hasn't got' is the baby Mary, on God's instruction, has just stolen: 'All right, all right. I got him from Safeways. I got him from Safeways in Lewisham' (*W.* 269 – consumerism indeed!). At the chronological close of the novel (but not its actual ending), she, like so many of Swift's other characters, is in an institution, staring silently out of the window (*W.* 329–30). What we remember as we read this is that Tom's ancestor, Sarah Atkinson, incurably damaged by her husband Tom's jealousy, has done much the same for fifty-four years back in the nineteenth century. And herein lies the nub of the novel: in effect, the whole book is an attempt to 'explain' – a word that tolls throughout it – why Mary steals a baby from Safeways in Lewisham in 1980. But to do so demands a history that needs to become more and more inclusive, to recognise how history repeats itself, to regress further and further back. In the chapter entitled 'About the Question Why', Tom Crick muses to his history class: 'when – where – how do we stop asking why? How far back? When are we satisfied that we possess an Explanation (knowing it is not a complete explanation)?' (W. 107–8). How far back must you go to possess 'the whole story' (W. 133, 155, 317, title of chapter 50)? But – and this is a crux in the novel – however far back and however inclusive, 'the whole story' will only ever be partial – in two senses of that word: both incomplete and biased. It will be told by someone who has incomplete knowledge and a particular slant on the account they are giving. 'The whole story', in other words, will always be a story with 'holes' in it (it is no coincidence that chapter 7 is entitled 'Of Holes and Things'). A better way of writing the phrase would surely be: 'the (w)hole story'.

The novel is narrated by Tom Crick, either in the first person or in a 'focalized' third person (see Chapter 1, pp. 10–11). It is, therefore, 'his-story' as much as it is 'history', and, while not itself using that play on words, *Waterland* has the implications of it right at its centre. The narrative *donnée* of the novel is that Crick is substituting for the official History syllabus he is supposed to be teaching (on the French Revolution) his own 'his-story' in order to 'explain' why his wife has been arrested and locked up in a mental hospital for stealing a baby from Safeways' supermarket in Lewisham. Part of the controlled and engaging postmodernist self-reflexivity of this novel lies in the way Crick addresses his sixth-form audience (and thus, of course, his readers) as 'Children'; chapter 2, significantly entitled 'About the End of History', opens 'Children. Children, who will inherit the world [...] children, before whom I have stood for thirty-two years in order to unravel the mysteries of the past [...]' (W. 5). It is further exemplified by the way one chapter will end: 'let me tell you' – only to be completed by the title of the next chapter: 'About the Fens' (W. 8). Other instances of *Waterland*'s self-consciousness include repeated allusions to fairy tales – on the first page, for example, we have: 'Fairy-tale words; fairy-tale advice. But we lived in a fairy-tale place' (*W.* 1); its use of the classic fairy-tale opening: 'Once upon a time ...' (*W.* 7 and *passim*); the appearance on the second page of that strategically ambiguous phrase 'telling stories': 'My father [...] had a knack for telling stories. Made-up stories, true stories, soothing stories, warning stories; stories with a moral or with no point at all; believable stories and unbelievable stories; stories which were neither one thing nor the other' (*W.* 2). 'Telling stories', of course, can simply mean the act of narration, but it also means stories that are 'telling' (that is, having significant import), and again, as in 'tell-tale', passing on or betraying the secrets of others – with the implication that these may be fabrications, 'made-up stories'. Such self-consciousness, as we shall see, is itself an aspect of the novel's overall thematic and formal meaning.

In order to 'explain' the present, then, Tom Crick's 'his-story' must 'unravel the mysteries of the past', and thus go a long way back historically – theoretically, in infinite regression – in the (futile) search for a point of origin (it is in this context that we will find the relevance of the novel's inclusion of a 'Natural History' (*W.* 205) of the eel). In fact, the earliest date given in the novel is 695 AD, 'or thereabouts' (*W.* 18), when Saint Gunnhilda – who gives her name to the town of Gildsey, the focus of much of the past history in the novel – built herself a hermit's hut in the middle of a marsh, heard the voice of God, and founded a church there (many centuries later, in 1980, another local female character will also hear the voice of God). But the main part of *Waterland*'s historical narrative begins around the middle of the seventeenth century (see *W.* 11–12), outlining the history of the Atkinson and Crick families (Tom's ancestors); their involvement in draining, managing and farming the Fens; the growing prosperity and power of the Atkinsons as they found a brewery, build waterways, locks, docks and then railways; become mayors and MPs; and then in the years around the First World War go into terminal decline.

This last period (*c.*1909–22) is one of two central ones in the novel, not counting its 'present' (the other is the Second World War, especially 1943 – see below). The last of the male Atkinsons, Ernest, having failed to get into Parliament, turns his attention to perfecting strong ales, the final result of which is his ferociously intoxicating 'Coronation Ale' and the apparently concomitant burning-down of the Atkinson brewery in June 1911 (*W.* 170–8). Having protested unpopularly against the war in 1914, the incipiently insane Ernest goes into complete retirement in 1915 at the family home, Kessling Hall; and in April of that year, Tom tells us, 'my grandfather fell in love [...] with his daughter.[...] And there's nothing Platonic about it' (*W.* 219–20). The daughter is Helen Atkinson, the mother of Tom and his retarded 'potato-head' brother, Dick (*W.* 32). Kessling Hall is turned into 'a hospital for victims of the war' (*W.* 227), especially the shell-shocked 'mental cases' like Henry Crick, Tom's father, who is invalided out of the war in January 1918, where he meets Helen, who becomes a trainee auxiliary nurse in February 1919 (*W.* 224). Meanwhile, Ernest – 'like those poor soldier boys, his mind had become wounded too' (*W.* 228) – wants to have 'a child, a very special sort of child' (*W.* 227) by Helen, believing that 'only from out of this beauty will come a Saviour of the World' (*W.* 220, 229). Helen finally agrees, but also marries Henry Crick in August 1922, and 'tried hard by two men at the same time [...] to become pregnant. Though who would be the child's father would perhaps never become clear till the baby was born' (*W.* 230; an even more uncertain paternity will occur again in 1943). On the night of 25 September that year, Ernest writes a letter to his unborn son explaining who his father was and 'enjoining him to save the world, which was a place in dire need of saving' (*W.* 233), puts it in a black brass-bound chest together with his journals and twelve bottles of Coronation Ale (*W.* 233–4), and instructs Helen that, on his eighteenth birthday, Dick may be given the key to the chest to unlock its 'secret contents' (in other words, a key to 'that sealed-up domain', the past (*W.* 284) – which Tom's 'his-story' analogously appropriates). The following day, drunk on Coronation Ale, Ernest 'put [a] loaded shot-gun into his mouth, and pulled the trigger' (*W.* 235). Dick the potato-head is born in 1923 – the Saviour of the World. When Helen Atkinson dies on 25 January 1937, Dick inherits the key to the chest, opens it, drinks one bottle of ale, which makes him hopelessly drunk, hurls the empty bottle into the river (bottles in rivers are a recurrent structuring motif in the novel), and never again opens the chest until 'he realized how its contents might help him' (*W.* 289) – in

1943. It will be apparent from the page references above that this murky story is revealed quite late in the novel (chapter 30), and only after Tom has 'unlocked the past inside a black wooden chest ...' – itself an event narrated still later on (*W.* 320; chapter 48), even though it had 'actually' taken place in 1943. Only gradually and piecemeal, in other words, do we gather the materials for 'the whole story'.

As in *The Sweet Shop Owner*, the First World War is a determinate presence in shaping the world that follows it. *Waterland*, for example, makes an extended correlation between the flooded Fenlands in 1916–18 and another 'flat, rain-swept, water-logged land.[...] Who will not feel in this twentieth century of ours [...] the mud of Flanders sucking at his feet?' (*W.* 19). But while the 'good people' of Gildsey gradually 'forgot about the war [...] because that was the main point of their forgetfulness and the most awkward thing of all' (*W.* 221–2), others like Henry Crick, 'all [...] wounded in the mind' *W.* (226), 'couldn't forget ... And even twenty-five years later, when [...] bombers set the night sky rumbling [...] there's still a small core [...] still in the throes of the old war, still trying to forget ... [...] quite a few who can't forget what a mad place the world is' (*W.* 222). Pointedly, the opening words of the novel, spoken by Henry Crick, are 'And don't forget' (*W.* 1). More symbolic, perhaps, is the implication that Dick is a child of twentieth-century war (like Irene in *The Sweet Shop Owner* and Prentis in *Shuttlecock*). Of Ernest Atkinson's incestuous love for his daughter in 1915, the novel asks: 'what more could he do [...] now that, across the sea in France, the world was constructing a hell-on-earth, than cling [...] to some left-over fragment of paradise' (*W.* 219). Thus Dick, not unlike W. B. Yeats's 'rough beast' in his poem 'The Second Coming', becomes a product of his times and a travesty of 'the Saviour of the World' – which Mary's stolen (and 'second') baby in 1980 is also likened to: 'The baby who, as everyone knows, was sent by God. Who will save us all' (*W.* 329). And it is no coincidence that one of the possible fathers of Mary's 'first' (aborted) baby was Dick in 1943 – right in the middle of the Second World War.

The second key past moment in *Waterland*, then, is the Second World War. Chapter 24 opens with a brief scene-setting of the German occupation of France in July 1940, implying that this is the result of 'previous successive onslaughts [...] from across the Rhine' – most obviously the war of 1914–18 in which 'a million and a half Frenchmen had given their lives' (W. 180). Hence the First World War breeds the Second. The chapter then swiftly segues (thus replacing History with 'his-story') to a group of Fenland schoolchildren, including Tom and Dick Crick, Mary Metcalf and Freddie Parr, on the banks of the Hockwell Lode (a local waterway), who are daring each other to show their sexual parts. This is the scene in which Dick's monstrous erect 'dick' inside his swimming trunks first attracts Mary's 'rekindled, refired, curiosity' (W. 186–7), and Freddie Parr puts a live eel down her knickers. By August 1942 – the war is inserted in parentheses: '(defeat in the desert; the U-boat stranglehold)' (50) – Tom and Mary as 15-year-old adolescents are enthusiastically exploring each other sexually ('holes and things'). Mary, in particular, is described thus, in an important passage for one of the novel's principal themes:

> Mary itched. And this itch of Mary's was the itch of curiosity. In her fifteen-year-old body curiosity tickled and chafed, making her fidgety and roving-eyed. Curiosity drove her, beyond all restraint, to want to touch, witness, experience whatever was unknown and hidden from her. Do not smirk, children. Curiosity, which, with other things, distinguishes us from the animals, is an ingredient of love. Is a vital force. (W. 51)

I will return to the connection between 'curiosity' and 'love' later, but we may notice here the relationship of curiosity to that insistent question 'Why?', and the driving need for 'explanation', which we have seen earlier so obsesses Tom Crick, the history-man. So curious is Mary that she encourages Dick to fall in love with her, although whether she samples his 'penis of fabulous dimensions' (W. 50) remains a well-kept secret. But it is in the summer of 1943 – 'when the scales of war tip (victory in Africa, German withdrawals in the east)', and Tom is first reading Thomas Carlyle's *French Revolution* (W. 254–5) – that the novel's centrally determining events take place. On the night of 25–6 July, Freddie Parr appears to have drowned in the River Leem while drunk. However, 'A Bruise upon a Bruise' (chapter 5) and Tom's discovery floating in the river of 'A beer bottle. A bottle of thick dark brown glass, but not a sort of bottle that is seen any more around the Fens – or has been seen for over thirty years' (*W*. 39) convinces him that Dick has killed Freddie by getting him drunk on Coronation Ale, hitting him on the head with the empty bottle, and tipping him into the Leem. Later that day, Mary, who is by now pregnant and from whose face 'something's gone [...] Curiosity's gone' (*W*. 57), says to Tom: 'I told him it was Freddie. Dick killed Freddie Parr because he thought it was him. Which means we're to blame too' (*W*. 35). What Mary is telling Tom is that the father of her unborn baby was not Freddie, nor was it Dick: ' "because it was too big.[...] Too big." "To go in?" "Yes" ' (*W*. 58). Nearly 250 pages later, still in August 1943, while Mary is attempting to abort the baby herself, Tom's jealousy – and we might recall here Thomas Atkinson's 223 years earlier when he strikes the innocent Sarah – causes him to scream: 'It's Dick's, isn't it? All along. Dick's. Dick's!'; Mary replies: 'Not Dick's. Ours. Ours. You understand?' (*W*. 293–4). But does Tom 'understand', and will he ever *know* for certain? Earlier, reflecting on what Mary has told him about her relationship with Dick, Tom repeats: 'It's Mary's story.[...] It's Mary's story, pieced together and construed by me. So how can I be certain what really——?' (*W*. 248–9). Already familiar with Swift's trademark phrases, we can readily supply the missing word '——happened?'. Later, Tom returns to this: 'Or that's Mary's story. Because how did I know, how could I be a hundred per cent sure that when Mary said Dick's was too big, it really was too big? And that Mary hadn't proved to herself that it wasn't Too Big, in fact was just right [...]' (*W*. 262). But, of course, this is not 'Mary's story' at all (no 'her-story' here): it is very emphatically Tom's – 'his-story' – the irony being that he will never know who the 'real' father of Mary's baby was – and nor will the reader. So the central 'hole' at the centre of 'the whole story' will remain Mary's hole and who filled it with a tiny eel-like foetus. I will return to the significance of this for the novel 'as a whole', and for what it is claiming about history and stories.

Still in August of 1943, chapter 41 ends: 'So, children, since no fairy-tale is complete without one, let me tell you' ... 'About the Witch' (title of chapter 42). Because Mary's self-inflicted attempts at abortion have gone wrong, she and Tom visit Martha Clay, an old Fen-dweller and 'wise-woman' who lives in the middle of a marsh and 'who made potions and predictions

(or so it was claimed). And who also got rid of love-children...'
(*W.* 298). Martha aborts the 'love-child'; Mary 'screams and then
says she's the mother of God—', intoning 'HolyMaryMother-
ofGodHolyMaryMotherofGodHolyMaryMotherof—' (*W.* 307–8).
It will not be lost on the reader that 'Mary' is her own name as
well as that of the Virgin Mary, mother of Christ, and that later
in life she will try and replace her lost baby by stealing one from
a supermarket in south-east London, God having told her she
will have a child (*W.* 130, 269) – a baby 'Who will save us all' (*W.*
329). Significantly, too, Tom observes of the aborted foetus that
'in the pail is what the future's made of' (*W.* 308). While clearly a
reference to his and Mary's childless future and the theft, it is
also – if we see the foetus as once more a 'child of war'
(conceived in 1943) – symbolic of a 'future' that is in some way
already stillborn: loveless, consumerist, approaching 'the end of
history' as it waits in the shadow of nuclear holocaust, a future,
as Crick has remarked earlier, 'faced instead – with no future at
all' (*W.* 154). It is also significant that, when Tom and Price have
a drink in the pub, Tom refers to 'this founding president' of the
school's 'Holocaust Club' (*W.* 258), and the boy who dreams of
nuclear annihilation, as his son: 'He's my son' (*W.* 241). Is Price
the ironic replacement for that aborted foetus from the Second
World War, is he 'what the future's made of' as it lies in the
bottom of the pail, are he and his anomie the 'price' the world is
paying for its past history and the evasion ('forgetting') of what
it should have taught us? The pub conversation seems to
confirm this:

> 'And who says if we *are* around that we'll want to have children [...]
> Who says there's going to be any world to bring them into?' [...]
>   'Who says we'll want to bring children into whatever world there
> is?'
>   [...] (Yes, yes, it's our fault, Price. The old ones. We haven't been
> vigilant. We've let the world slip away. Should have saved it.) (*W.*
> 258)

The older generation has not 'saved the world', and the notion
should remind us, as Tom puts it elsewhere, that there are 'no
short cuts to Salvation, no recipe for a New World' (*W.* 108), that
Dick ('Saviour of the World') and Mary's stolen baby ('Who will
save us all') are the delusions of religious insanity. But no more
have the 'realistic' historians like Tom Crick 'saved the world'.

Earlier in the scene with Price, Tom silently muses on his experience of being in Germany after the war in 1946: 'All that rubble.[...] Things looked dark then and they do now. In 1946 I had a vision of the world in ruins.[...] And now here you are, Price, in 1980, with your skull-face and your Holocaust Club, saying the world may not have much longer – and you're not much younger than I was then' (W. 239–40). 'The old ones' have failed their son Price by 'forgetting', by letting the world 'slip away'.

Back in 1943, Tom tips the aborted foetus into the River Ouse (W. 317), but, like the Ouse eels and like Dick, as we shall see, the cyclical nature of history means that the past will return – for good or ill. When Dick learns about the loss of Mary's baby, he gets the key to his (grand)father's chest – 'as if it's the key to all the riddles of life' (W. 319) – and asks Tom to read the letter that explains who his parents were. Tom, echoing Quinn in *Shuttlecock*, thinks: 'Better not to learn. Better never to know. But once you've ...' – you can't get rid of knowledge, and now 'Dick knows' (W. 324). He goes off on his motor-bike to the dredger where he works carrying a sack containing the remaining ten bottles of Coronation Ale. Tom and his father follow him, watch him drink the bottles of beer, then try to persuade a local boatman to row out to the dredger but are faced with 'the mammoth task of explanation' as to why Dick is where he is doing what he is (W. 351). Tom makes the attempt: 'I review in my mind a dozen possible starting-points [...] I realize the utter impossibility of encapsulating, in the space of a moment, the causes of my brother's (my whose?) presence [...] on the *Rosa II*. I settle for succinct fabrication. "He's gone barmy"' (W. 351). In the final chapter of the novel, this is a striking piece of self-reflexivity, for the whole book has been concerned to show the 'utter impossibility' of knowing where to start ('How far back?') in trying to tell that other 'utter impossibility', 'the whole story'. As the novel itself proves, 'succinct fabrication' is about as near 'the truth' as you are likely to get.

Late on in this final chapter, the Allied twenty-four-hour bombing of German cities is marginally alluded to (W. 355) – as though the war is the remote but determinate context for the personal 'his-story' being recounted. As Henry and Tom approach the dredger, 'the saviour of the world' dives off the boat, disappears under water (just as he had done three years before in the diving competition at Hockwell Lock), and presumably drowns. I say 'presumably', because on that previous occasion he resurfaces minutes later some hundred yards down the river (*W.* 190) – without the huge erection he had had when he dived in. So that Tom wonders whether Dick 'has achieved [...] some satisfaction, some ecstasy [...] and has already—? So that, even now, twisting strands of Dick's congealed seed are floating down towards [...] the sea ...' (*W.* 190–1). Echoing this, the penultimate paragraph of the novel ends: 'He's on his way. Obeying instinct. Returning. The Ouse flows to the sea ' (*W.* 357). If we recall the eel's mysterious life cycle, the origin of which no one has ever discovered, then 'returning' can imply both a return *to* source and the possibility of returning *from* it. Hence, might we expect Dick's 'second coming' (in both senses of the term)? The final lines of the novel hint at this, while also gathering up resonant motifs from across 'the whole story': ' "Someone best explain." We trip over empty bottles. Peer from the rails. Ribbons of mist. Obscurity. On the bank in the thickening dusk, in the will-o'-the-wisp dusk, abandoned but vigilant, a motor-cycle' (*W.* 358). The injunction to 'explain' effectively takes us back to the start of the novel, the whole of which has been seeking to do just that, while early on, the reader has indeed tripped over 'empty bottles' (*W.* 4) before he or she has any sense of their significance. 'Mist', 'obscurity', 'thickening dusk' all suggest the murkiness of trying to see 'what really happened', of peering blindly into 'the mysteries of the past', while a 'will-o'-the-wisp' is metaphorically something that is impossible to reach or catch – like the truth, for example, about the origins of the eel, of Dick, and of Mary's baby. Finally, we may note that odd word 'vigilant' used about a motor cycle in the final line: does it mean that, living in expectation, it is looking out for the 'return', the 'second coming', of its owner? But that would be another story, for this is where *Waterland* the novel – but not its chronology – ends: in late August 1943.

In the novel's 'present', Tom Crick's school is 'cutting history' (*W.* 5, 21 – chapter 2 is entitled 'About the End of History'), the postmodern resonances of which I shall return to shortly. The headteacher, Lewis, an apparatchik of the new managerialist society, who is under pressure to provide only subjects with 'practical relevance to today's real world' (*W.* 22) and who believes that 'History breeds pessimism' (*W.* 154), is about to make Crick redundant. As we know, much of the novel's narrative comprises Tom's substitution of 'his-story' for the official History syllabus ('turning your lessons into these – story-telling sessions' (*W.* 153)). His audience comprises sixth-formers, but his principal addressee – both directly and often silently – is Price, President of the Holocaust Club and Crick's 'son' (see above, p. 33). It is Price, the spokesperson for postmodern youth, who believes that 'What matters [...] is the here and now. Not the past. The here and now – and the future' (*W.* 6), and that 'The only important thing about history [...] is that it's got to the point where it's probably about to end' (*W.* 7, 154). Crick responds in defence of *historia* by offering his 'fairy-tale' ('Once upon a time'): 'Your history teacher wishes to give you the complete and final version ...' (*W.* 7–8). Swift's ellipses are always 'telling'.

What Price represents is a world in which reality is displaced by simulacra, images, fantasies and deceptions, 'curiosity' is no more, and history (as much a sense of futurity as a sense of the past) seems about to end in the face of the wholesale destruction of humanity and civilization incident on nuclear holocaust – the anticipation of which, as Martin Amis has suggested, 'is the only experience of nuclear war that anyone is going to get'.[3] Such a subliminal acceptance of 'the End of History', postmodern theorists claim, leads to a sense only of a continuous present – what Price calls 'the here and now' – a present that perceives no point in political, moral or cultural endeavour or agency, and therefore can have no meaningful sense of a future. Crick asks his headteacher: 'what does education do, what does it have to offer, when deprived of its necessary partner, the future, and faced instead with – no future at all?' (*W.* 154). This is posed in the context of Tom telling Lewis about his class's 'nuclear nightmares' (*W.* 195): 'Nine out of sixteen said they've dreamt of nuclear war. In several cases a recurring nightmare. They dream about the end of the world' (*W.* 153), but the most telling is the dream Price describes to Crick in the pub (significantly it comprises the whole of chapter 40 and is under one page long – such short chapters in Swift's fiction invariably seem to signal their centrality to the novel's overall themes). A nuclear blast has just taken place:

they announce it on the telly. You know: you've got four minutes ...
But no one seems to notice. No one moves. My Dad's snoring in his
chair. I'm screaming. My mum just sits there wanting to know
what's happened to *Crossroads* ... all the buildings go red-hot and
then they go white and all the people go red too and white ... (You
couldn't see that – you'd be dead. Stupid).[...] Suicide pills, sir. We sit
round and all take them together ... (*W*. 296–7)

And during Lewis's farewell speech to Crick, when his
'Children' demonstrate against the 'cutting of history' and
Tom's forced retirement (the Holocaust Club has already been
banned as an 'uneducational activity'), their repeated chant is
'Fear is here! Fear is here!' (*W*. 333). This, the novel seems to
propose, is 'the postmodern condition'.

What Crick (with Swift behind him?) offers as the antidote to
such a condition, and as central to our humanity and
civilization, is *historia*: at once as history and story. A year
before Jean-François Lyotard's *The Postmodern Condition* (1979)
was translated into English (1984), *Waterland* presents 'History
itself' as 'the Grand Narrative, the filler of vacuums, the
dispeller of fears of the dark' (*W*. 62). Later, in conversation
with Price about the necessity of teaching history – and indeed
the telling of 'his-stories' – Crick says: 'All right, so it's all a
struggle to preserve an artifice. It's all a struggle to make things
not seem meaningless. All a fight against fear.[...] It helps to
drive out fear.[...] It helps to eliminate fear' (*W*. 241); and, in the
pivotal chapter 'About the Question Why', he claims that 'what
history teaches us is to avoid illusion and make-believe, to lay
aside dreams, moonshine, cure-alls, wonder-workings, pie-in-
the-sky – to be realistic' (*W*. 108). 'Histories' represent asking 'the
Question Why': they 'demand of history an Explanation' (*W*. 62),
allow 'curiosity' full rein, seek knowledge (*historia* – 'learning by
inquiry'), defeat 'forgetting', want to know 'what really
happened', 'the whole truth', 'the whole story' – even if, as we
shall see, we have to accept ultimate failure in trying to do so.
And they help us, as Crick says above, to be 'realistic' (in answer
to Lewis's belief that 'History breeds pessimism', Tom replies:
'Or realism. Or realism' (*W*. 155)).

Another term for 'the Here and Now' in the novel's scheme
of things is 'Reality' – of which, as T. S. Eliot put it, 'human kind
cannot bear very much',[4] and *Waterland* seems to agree. 'Reality'

is the raw lived experience of the moment: it is the Terror during the French Revolution ('Reality made plain. Reality with no nonsense. Reality cut down to size. Reality minus a few heads' (W. 206)); it is Freddie Parr's murder ('Reality's already imposed itself in the form of a sodden corpse' (W. 263)); it is the two world wars; it is Mary's teenage pregnancy and abortion; it is her stealing of the baby forty years later ('Reality's so strange, so strange and unexpected' (W. 25)). It is 'History', in other words, as it is happening, what Thomas Carlyle once called the 'Chaos of Being'. [5] What *historia* does, conversely – 'this cumbersome but precious bag of clues called History' (W. 106) – is help us to become 'realistic', to shape and order events so that they become meaningful, to 'explain' and thus 'understand'; and, in so doing, it works against the insanities of war, revolution, superstition and religion ('dreams, moonshine, cure-alls, wonder-workings, pie-in-the-sky': Dick as 'Saviour of the World'; Mary's 'love-affair with God'). But being 'realistic' is also to recognize and acknowledge the limits of *historia*. For a start, history (like rivers and eels) seems to go in circles:

> It goes in two directions at once. It goes backwards as it goes forwards.[...] It cannot be denied, children, that the great so-called forward movements of civilization [...] have invariably brought with them an accompanying regression.[...] No wonder we move in circles. (W. 135–6)

Furthermore, the claim that History helps us 'To learn (the history master's hoary stand-by) lessons from our mistakes so it will be better in future ...' (W. 107) is itself a myth: 'Why is it that every so often history demands a bloodbath, a holocaust, an Armageddon? And why is it that every time the time before has taught us nothing?' (W. 141). In his argument with Lewis, Tom believes that children ('Heirs of the future, vessels of hope') will 'grow up pretty quickly to be like their parents [...] make the same mistakes as their parents, that the same old things will repeat themselves.[...] It's what history tells them [...]' (W. 240). However, he adds importantly: 'But if [...] they've struggled not to be like them, if they've tried [...] and so prevented things slipping. If they haven't let the world get any *worse* ——?'. Do we complete the final sentence here with: 'then that's about all we can hope for'?

Equally, a 'realistic' view of history will accept that any explanation it gives is partial: somebody will be telling it from a particular perspective and it will be incomplete:

> history is that impossible thing: the attempt to give an account, with incomplete knowedge, of actions themselves undertaken with incomplete knowledge. So that it teaches us no short-cuts to Salvation, no recipe for a New World, only the dogged and patient art of making do. I taught you that by forever attempting to explain we may come, not to an Explanation, but to a knowledge of the limits of our power to explain. (W. 108)

This is another crucial statement, and, tied to that above about 'not letting the world get any *worse*', will feature centrally in my conclusion here. Furthermore, exploiting its etymological origins, 'History' is presented as no more than a branch of storytelling – a *narrative* – which nevertheless purports to be factual (in this, the novel colludes with much influential thinking in contemporary academic historiography), a product of imagination and susceptible to subjective interpretation. During an exchange between Crick and Price, the latter asks:

> 'Should we be writing this down, sir? The French Revolution never really happened. It only happened in the imagination.' [...] 'I'm speculating, it's true, Price. But we're all free to interpret.' 'You mean, so we can find whatever meaning we like in history?' (But actually I do believe that.... History: a lucky dip of meanings. Events elude meaning, but we look for meanings. Another definition of Man: the animal who craves meaning – but knows –). (W. 140)

Again the final hanging sentence end ('– he'll never find it'?). So history, as Price would have it, is not much more than a fairy tale itself. But at one point, Crick interrupts his own story by saying:

> There are times when we have to disentangle history from fairy-tale.[...] History [...] only wants to know the facts. History, if it is to keep on constructing its road into the future, must do so on solid ground. At all costs let us avoid mystery-making and speculation, secrets and idle gossip. And, for God's sake, nothing supernatural. And above all, let us not tell *stories*.[...] Let us get back to solid ground ... (W. 86)

This prefaces a section that purports to be giving a factual account of the rising power and prosperity of the Atkinson family after the death of old Tom, but that is constantly undercut by interpolations of local rumour and superstition about the mad, silent Sarah sitting at her window for fifty-four years: 'Sarah's work perhaps. But let us keep to the facts' (W. 87); 'Rumour is unleashed with the floodwater' (W. 101); 'Do not ghosts prove – even rumours, whispers, stories of ghosts – that the past clings ...' (W. 103). The point is – as the physical motif of the novel's environment indicates (the Fens are 'reclaimed land, land that was once water, and which, even today, is not quite solid' (W. 8)) – that there is no 'solid ground' on which to build a 'road into the future', no 'facts' that are not in one way or another fabricated, no history of which 'a good half' is not, in Price's phrase, 'make-believe' (W. 140), nothing that is not constructed within and as *stories*. And 'this historical method, this explanation-hunting', while being 'a way of getting at the truth', may also be 'a way of coming up with just another story, a way of giving reality the slip' (W. 263). For, despite their importance to human beings, stories themselves are problematic: malicious and superstitious ('Some said that Martha Clay was a witch ... But let's keep clear of fairy-tales' (W. 11); full of 'holes' (who fathered Mary's baby? Where is 'her-story'?); susceptible to variation ('End of story.[...] That can't be the end.[...] Very well. No end of story' (W. 109)); and economical with the truth ('I settle for succinct fabrication' (W. 351)). But it is the ironic ambiguity in that phrase above, 'giving reality the slip', that lies at the heart of *Waterland*, and that will allow me now to bring some threads together in conclusion.

The four main threads that weave in and out of the texture of the novel are: *historia*, curiosity, civilization and love. 'Reality', 'the Here and Now', as we have heard, is 'the human condition': the relentless historical process of meaningless human tragedy and farce that individuals experience as 'the present'. In Swift's postmodern world, this present comprises the determinate consequences of two world wars, the threat of nuclear holocaust, a technological consumerist society where 'a fruit machine vomits. The space invaders close in' (W. 259), where 'fear' or 'pie-in-the-sky' religion have replaced love, where the 'end of history' is at hand, and the end of the world is nigh. This is the 'reality' that must, in some way, be 'given the slip'. When Crick is explaining to Price how he came to be a history teacher, he cites his experience of post-war Germany in 1946 as the reason: because he 'made the discovery that this thing called civilization [...] is precious. An artifice – so easily knocked down – but precious' (*W.* 239–40). He knows that the 'reality' is his 'vision of the world in ruins' (*W.* 240), but against it he pits *historia* – which he also knows is artificial, vulnerable and problematic – and *historia* means the retention of 'curiosity' at all costs. He repeats his correlation of curiosity and 'love' (see above, p. 31) very much later in the novel:

> Children, be curious. Nothing is worse [...] than when curiosity stops. Nothing is more repressive than the repression of curiosity. *Curiosity begets love.* It weds us to the world.[...] People die when curiosity goes. People have to find out, people have to know. How can there be any true revolution till we know what we're made of? (*W.* 206; emphasis added)

And 'knowing what we're made of' means 'To know that what we are is what we are because our past has determined it' (*W.* 107). History and story – or better, both as one: *historia* – artificial as they may be, full of holes, incomplete in explanation, never able to go far enough back, nevertheless represent 'curiosity', the search for 'meaning', and hence 'civilization':

> Children, there's this thing called civilization. It's built of hopes and dreams. It's only an idea. It's not real. It's artificial.[...] It breaks easily.[...] And no one ever said it would last for ever.[...] There's this thing called progress. But it doesn't progress, it doesn't go anywhere. Because as progress progresses the world can *slip away.* It's progress if you can stop *the world slipping away.* My humble model for progress is the reclamation of land. Which is repeatedly, never-endingly retrieving what is lost. (*W.* 336; emphases added)

And so we come full circle, for the reclaimed land of the Fens is formed by 'silt', 'which demolishes as it builds; which is simultaneous accretion and erosion; neither progress nor decay' (*W.* 9): 'Strictly speaking, [the Fens] are never reclaimed, only being reclaimed' (*W.* 10). So, too, the novel says, with human history and story: always seeking to reclaim the past in order to give meaning to the present, to shore up a civilization that 'breaks easily' and is constantly in danger of 'slipping away' (no 'solid ground' or 'progress' here) – and especially in the present where 'the end of the world came back again [...] as something the world had fashioned for itself all the time it was growing up' (*W.* 336). A 'reality', 'the Here and Now', overdetermined by the prospect of nuclear catastrophe and the sense of a futureless future that renders human agency pointless, is surely one version of 'the end of the world', and coterminous with it is 'the end of history' – a central notion in defining the postmodern mindset. But Crick has earlier posited that

> only animals live entirely in the Here and Now. Only nature knows neither memory nor history. But man [...] is the story-telling animal. Wherever he goes he wants to leave behind not a chaotic wake, not an empty space, but the comforting marker-buoys and trail-signs of stories. He has to go on telling stories, he has to keep on making them up. As long as there's a story, it's all right. (*W.* 62–3)

And he later adds: 'when the world is about to end there'll be no more reality, only stories. All that will be left to us will be stories. We'll sit down, in our shelter, and tell stories, like poor Scheherazade, hoping it will never ...' (*W.* 298).

In the absence of any other effective value system, *Waterland* seems to be saying, 'telling stories'– which can simultaneously stop 'the world slipping away' (prevent 'forgetting') and 'give reality the slip' (see beyond 'the Here and Now') – are/is our only lifeline. That the novel makes such an affirmation so brilliantly itself should not, however, blind us to its own bleak postmodern affiliations. It may be an exemplary instance of what Linda Hutcheon has called 'historiographic metafiction' (see Introduction, p. 5) in its self-reflexive rebuttal of the claims made by both conventional History and fictional Realism to be truth-telling discourses. But recuperating *historia* so persuasively from them does not obscure the fact that in 'the present' of the novel Price's 'nuclear nightmares' have not been exorcised; Lewis is 'cutting history' on behalf of something called 'the real world'; Mary is insane and silent in an institution; and Tom Crick is both redundant and without her ('He can't sleep. His bed's empty and marooned in a black sea' (*W.* 331)). Where, one wonders, in this bereft postmodern present, is even that 'love' which 'curiosity begets' and which 'weds us to the world', that minimal reflex of a new humanism which *Waterland* seems to want to promote? It is perhaps articulated most indicatively when Dick asks his father where babies come from ('They come

42

from love, Dick. They're made with Love'): 'Lu-love', he says –
and the novel comments: 'Another difficult word' (*W*. 257).
Given the fate of Mary's baby and all that follows from it, given
Dick – an incestuously conceived potato-head 'love-child'
destined to be 'the Saviour of the World' – and given Tom's
final farewell to Mary in her asylum: 'Mary. Lu-love. Lu-love' (*W*.
331), 'love' does indeed seem to be 'a difficult word'. We will
follow its course with interest in the novels to come.

3

Out of This World

In his next novel after *Waterland*, the undeservedly less admired *Out of This World*, Graham Swift again attempts a large-scale history of the twentieth century principally in terms of its warfare. This is told by way of the family history of the Beeches, whose wealth is founded on armaments manufacture, developed especially by the one-armed father, Robert Beech, VC (whose 'life spanned the full galloping gamut of the twentieth century' (*OTW* 11)), and disowned by his son Harry, one of the novel's two main narrative voices. Harry becomes first an aerial photographer with the RAF in the Second World War and then a war photographer in all the trouble spots of the post-war world. In 1972, ten years before the novel opens, he has given up this career after his father is blown to pieces by a bomb planted in his car by the IRA, although he continues to do some flying and photography. Harry's Greek wife, Anna, has been killed in an air crash years earlier, leaving Sophie, Harry's only child and the other main narrative voice in the novel. She is increasingly alienated from her often absent father, and cuts herself off from him totally after her beloved grandfather's death, seeing Harry's moral nullity as somehow implicated in that event. When the novel opens ('April 1982' – this time, the date of 'the present' is given a page to itself at the beginning of the book, and April, as we shall see, seems to have some talismanic significance for Swift), Sophie, who lives in New York with her travel-agent husband, Joe, and is undergoing psychoanalysis, is on an aeroplane with her 9-year-old twin sons flying to England to make a reconciliation with Harry (*OTW* 201–2). Harry, aged just 64 and also flying in a Cessna light aircraft in the absolute present of the novel (*OTW* 38-9, 189), is living in a cottage in Wiltshire, having fallen in love with a 23-year-old woman, Jenny, who is pregnant with their child and whom he has left on the ground at the airfield. The novel is primarily narrated by way of the fragmentary 'confessions' of Harry and Sophie in 1982: Harry's, a mental apologia to Sophie to which we are party, while Sophie's is to Dr Klein, her psychiatrist. However, once again, the chronological order of the events narrated is so dislocated by the text that the 'actuality' of what has happened in the family past, which 'explains' the present, emerges gradually and implicitly only as the novel proceeds – as, too, does the relationship of that past to major historical events of the twentieth century.

A brief account of the novel's underlying – and again precise – chronology may, therefore, be in order. The earliest date mentioned is 1709, when Hyfield House, which Robert Beech buys in 1923 (*OTW* 198), was originally built: 'The genuine, historical, English thing.[...] The real, authentic country-house experience' (*OTW* 65) – all words that the novel will call into question. But the main period covered by the novel – and we grow accustomed to this in Swift's fiction – is from the First World War to 'the present'. Robert Beech is a Sandhurst cadet 'circa 1916' (*OTW* 90), who marries Harry's mother in April 1917 (*OTW* 198 – note the month again). On 27 March 1918, Harry is born and his mother dies in childbirth (*OTW* 29); three days later (*OTW* 197), already aware of what has happened, Robert (whose two brothers have already been killed in the war) is standing in a trench on the Western Front when a live grenade lands less than a foot away from where his commanding officer lies wounded; Robert picks it up and is about to throw it clear when it explodes and blows off his arm (*OTW* 195). For this act of bravery, he is awarded the Victoria Cross, but as we discover, and echoing *Shuttlecock*, all may not be as it seems. Robert blames his son for his wife's death, and they lead an estranged life; but ten years later, on the tenth anniversary of the Armistice, Robert takes Harry on an aeroplane trip that initiates Harry's love of flying. To his father's bitter disappointment, Harry shows no inclination to join the family firm, so that in the summer of 1944 (*OTW* 47) Frank Irving – with whom Harry's wife, Anna, is later to have an affair – joins BMC and gradually takes Harry's place as Robert's surrogate 'son'. The same year, Harry, who has joined the RAF, becomes an aerial war photographer covering the Allied destruction of German cities as the Second World War grinds towards its close. And in 1946, he is sent to Nuremberg to cover the end of the Nazi war trials (*OTW* 101), where, in 'that city of guilt and grief and retribution' (*OTW* 133), he falls in love with and immediately marries a Greek girl, Anna (*OTW* 135). Two days later, he is taking photos of the crowd waiting outside the prison walls where the Nazis are being executed (*OTW* 103).

'Cut' – as Harry's narrative in the novel regularly says – to 1953, the year of the Coronation of Queen Elizabeth II, which Joe, Sophie's husband, watches on the family's new TV in preference to 'catching a bus to Westminster and watching *the real thing*' (*OTW* 151; emphasis added) – as we shall see, this now familiar phrase lies at the heart of the novel's concern with the substitution of 'images' or simulacra for 'the real thing', whatever that may be. On holiday in Cornwall with Frank Irving's family the same summer, Harry sees his wife Anna and Frank (Harry's surrogate once more) making love (*OTW* 166–7); Anna becomes pregnant (it couldn't be Harry's – he was 'away so much [...] Taking pictures' (*OTW* 168–9)); she is called back to Greece in the autumn to see her dying uncle; and is killed in a plane crash on Mount Olympus (*OTW* 30–2). The motherless Sophie (effectively fatherless, too, since Harry is 'away so much [...] Taking pictures') then lives with her grandfather at Hyfield House.

'Cut' to 1969: Harry is just back in England from Vietnam and is watching the first Apollo moon landings with his father: 'nothing was real. The moon over English elm trees wasn't real, and [nor were] men walking on the moon' (*OTW* 12). Significantly, the astronauts – 'those moon-men, mission-controlled men in their absurd outfits' – remind him of the marines he patrolled with in Vietnam: 'Just walking hardware too' whose outfits 'didn't show if there was a *real man* inside' (13; emphasis added; robotic behaviour is a feature of the novel's world). Three years after this, on 23 April 1972 (*OTW* 68; note the month), Robert Beech's Daimler is blown up by the IRA at Hyfield House with himself and his chauffeur inside while Harry and the pregnant Sophie are in the house. Robert's funeral takes place on 3 May 1972, and that is the last time Sophie has had any contact with her father (*OTW* 33). Harry gives up war photography, but in 1973 becomes a peacetime aerial photographer taking pictures of prehistoric monuments discernible beneath the Wiltshire landscape. And finally we are back in the present of April 1982, where another significant event is well underway: the Falklands War – which 'is going to be the TV event of the year' (*OTW* 185). However, it is worth noting that, as with others of Swift's works, the novel itself actually begins in 1969, with Harry remembering Vietnam and the Apollo astronauts' moon-walk, and ends back in 1928 when his father takes him on an aeroplane flight. As we have come to expect, 'the present' is always bracketed by the past – and a past imbued with warfare. As Harry reflects on the First World War – that 'horrific collision of the antiquated and the modern' (*OTW* 196) – it was 'only the terrible prototype [...] of further collisions that would go on happening, in even more polarized and grotesque forms' (*OTW* 196). With devastating irony, however, the last lines of the novel imply Harry's liberation in 1928 from Robert's world ('his feet [...] so to speak [...] still caught in the mud' (of Flanders)): 'And I was being lifted up and away, out of his world, out of the age of mud, out of that brown, obscure age, into the age of air' (*OTW* 208). But 'the age of air', as Harry is to discover, would include the bombing of 'Hamburg, Bremen, Cologne, Essen, Düsseldorf, Berlin' (*OTW* 47), and the 'unreality' of 'those robot-men, clones of NASA technology' (*OTW* 13): men on the moon.

Like *Waterland*, then, *Out of This World* is an attempt to present a fictional history of the twentieth century, once again emphasizing the dehumanization implicit in war and its contaminations. All the main characters have had their emotional and moral lives atrophied by association with violence in one way or another, and the novel is an account by flashbacks of that process. The one-armed 'hero', Robert Beech, finally tells Harry during their conversation in 1969 what his own father said to him shortly before he died in 1922: ' "I'm proud of you, Bob." And do you know what he meant by that? He meant I was a damn good mascot.[...] I was a walking asset' (*OTW* 199); and his artificial arm – or rather the nine developing models he owns over the years – is emblematic of this (his joke is that he is indeed 'in the arms business' (*OTW* 199)). This 'stash of nine artificial arms' is kept by Harry as 'a miniature museum of prosthetic technology', which he says, pointedly, is 'like an index of the twentieth century' (*OTW* 199–200). One crucial aspect of this 'index' is that 'the later ones look like nothing human, but actually simulate the function of an arm' (*OTW* 200); we might catch an echo in 'nothing human' here of the Bionic Man in *Shuttlecock* who 'bears no relation to anything natural' – whilst another joke of Robert's is: 'I make a good robot, don't I?' (*OTW* 67). Earlier, when the young Sophie asks her grandfather what had happened to his 'real' arm, he replies 'Oh, I swapped it for a medal' (*OTW* 62) – in other words, for a replica of bravery. These 'simulations' – a synonym for 'simulacra' – are, of course, substitutes for 'the real thing' and relate to a central theme of the novel.

Other characters also bear the scars of war: most obviously Harry, who is born in March 1918, when the last major German offensive of the First World War began – thus joining Irene in *The Sweet Shop Owner*, Prentis in *Shuttlecock*, Dick and Price in *Waterland*, as a 'child of war'; and who leads a loveless childhood and adolescence. Sophie may have spent an idyllic childhood at the Queen Anne Hyfield House, which was like 'tak[ing] a break from the twentieth century', but she now realizes that this refuge in a 'make-believe' past was only a fairy tale (her own story beginning with that now familiar Swiftian trope: 'Once upon a time, in the reign of good Queen Anne ...' (*OTW* 65–6)); and she reminds herself not to be 'fooled by all this, don't be taken in, remember what all this is made of' (*OTW* 62). For what Hyfield House – 'the genuine, historical, English thing' – really is is 'the unofficial headquarters of BMC', what Harry calls 'the arsenal' (*OTW* 62), so that Sophie's 'refuge' is in effect 'made of' money from the manufacture and sale of armaments (not unlike the tainted money as 'converted history' that Dorothy inherits in *The Sweet Shop Owner*). The reasons, too, for Sophie's need of the analyst's couch in New York are the violent death of her grandfather, which she witnesses when pregnant with the twins ('I think I stopped loving anyone then' (*OTW* 138)), and the alienation she feels from her 'detached' war-photographer father, of one of whose photographs – 'They called it "that famous shot"' – she says: 'I didn't know which was worse, that the world contained such things or that my father had taken that picture' (*OTW* 78). Her resulting anomie leads to infidelity to Joe – 'just cheap, quick, mindless screws to make me forget I was anybody' (*OTW* 96): 'Your mummy fucks around.... Gets fucked. Is all fucked-up' (*OTW* 139). Sophie, in other words, has become a loveless sexual robot – rather like Prentis in *Shuttlecock*. Equally, Harry's dead wife Anna, in the sole section of the novel that she narrates, describes her young life in war-ravaged Greece (again, her two brothers were killed in the Second World War (*OTW* 134)), and then in Nuremberg, where she meets Harry in 1946, seeing herself as 'one of the world's walking wounded': 'I understood what the war had done to me. It had made me a thick-skinned, old-young thing.' So that the 'tough little bitch ... somewhere inside me' (*OTW* 174) would later coolly conduct 'a tactical affair' (*OTW* 174) with Robert Beech's substitute 'son', Frank: as with so many of Swift's characters, it is the capacity for love that war has destroyed in Anna. And even Joe, in the one section he too is given to narrate, speculates about his conception: 'Some unthinkable night in the Blitz? Some topsy-turvy moment in the Anderson shelter when the bombs were getting close ... and they thought, if not now, then maybe never? I was a war baby. June 1941' (*OTW* 156). There are a lot of 'war babies' in Swift's fiction.

The dehumanizing process is also articulated in the imagery the novel uses. One example is Sophie's account of seducing a plumber in New York: 'I put my hand on his cock, hard as a pistol' (*OTW* 18); another is her obsessive refusal to let her boys have toy guns because she fears they lead to 'the real thing' (*OTW* 73), implying, of course, that the simulacrum is as dangerous as the real gun. This now familiar Swiftian theme of a blurring of real and unreal, image and thing, is central to *Out of This World*, for the other things Sophie will not have in the house are cameras, since in her mind they are analogous to guns: 'You can shoot with both. You can load and aim with both' (*OTW* 77). I have noted above the devastating effect Harry's 'famous *shot*' (emphasis added) has had on her, but this motif is reiterated elsewhere in the novel: cameramen at Robert Beech's funeral were 'positioned like snipers', 'waiting in full ambush. Primed and loaded', and then 'they all fired away. Zap! Zap! Zap!' (*OTW* 84–5), 'Snap shots! Ha! Ha!' (*OTW* 86), their flash bulbs also being likened to 'pistol shots' (*OTW* 93). What this correlation of guns and cameras signals, however, is that in Swift's novel the dominant motif of twentieth-century alienation is its own mode of self-representation or self-knowing: photography. This is at once a form of 'mechanical' dehumanization, a form of truth-telling, a form of lying – and an analogy, in all these respects, for the novel's own attempts to 'capture' how it was, to offer a 'portrait' of a family, to 'record' twentieth-century reality. Indeed, the novel as a whole is a meditation on the truthfulness or not of representation, using photography and other forms of 'picturing', especially TV and film, as its focus.

As a child, Harry is given a camera by his father, and significantly 'receive[s] it like an emblem of guilt' (*OTW* 30). Later, as an RAF photographer, he registers 'the marks of destruction' that were 'Hamburg, Bremen, Cologne, Essen, Düsseldorf, Berlin' (*OTW* 47), and, after 'covering' the Nuremberg trials, Harry becomes a famous war-photographer in Algiers, Stanleyville, the Congo, Vietnam, Belfast, Alabama – always taking the 'grieving mother'; the 'anguished buddies'; the 'lacerated victim'; the 'blurred scream for help' (*OTW* 115–18). He becomes 'this new kind of hero [...] a hero without a gun [...] but flinching at nothing to bring back the truth'. Or is he rather, he wonders, a 'freak', a 'sicko', who 'calmly (calmly!)' and 'voluntarily' 'snaps' photographs of 'the maimed and dying and desperate' (*OTW* 118)? Later again, living in rural retreat, in love with Jenny, and working as a peacetime aerial photographer, his photographs of Bronze Age field-systems in fact show up Ministry of Defence (MOD) installations. Half of the rural counties of South-West England 'are military property. MOD. Keep Out. Not countryside any more – camouflage', and Harry comments: 'I know this landscape is a lie' (*OTW* 194). All this, of course, is in one sense a 'true' representation of twentieth-century experience, which does indeed 'lie', dehumanize and brutalize; and, as Harry says: 'Someone has to be a witness, someone has to to see. And tell? And tell?' (*OTW* 163; I will return to 'telling' later). But the *process* of 'seeing', too, is itself dehumanizing, despite the pretence of merely being 'witness, observer, neutral party, floating pair of eyes' (*OTW* 70). The moment at which this process is most complete in Harry's case, and Sophie is finally alienated from him, is when she catches him 'covering' his father's death:

He was like a man sleep-walking, not knowing how he could be doing what he was doing, as if it were all part of some deep, ingrained reflex. But just for a moment I saw this look on his face of deadly concentration. He hadn't seen me first because he'd been looking elsewhere, and his eyes had been jammed up against a camera. (*OTW* 111–12)

Harry has become robotic: the creature of his own camera.

But the question *Out of This World* poses – as the novel itself tries to expose the secrets and lies of the family history, to tell the truth behind the reified and blank postures of the main characters – is: just how true is this 'representation', how 'neutral' and objective is it ever? From initially believing that 'the camera doesn't manufacture' (*OTW* 13); that a news photographer 'can't select the news'; that 'the great value of photography [is] its actuality'; that there is 'nothing of yourself' in the photograph' (*OTW* 117–18), Harry begins to change his views. First, there is his recognition that the wartime authorities 'buried' half his pictures: 'you aren't supposed to see, let alone put on visual record, *those* things' (*OTW* 49) – 'even if they were, according to my brief, "authentic visual records of the air war"' (*OTW* 105). Later, these 'are released and become aestheticized as examples of his '"famous" early shots' (*OTW* 105). But watching the moon landing in 1969, and just back from Vietnam, he now reflects: 'the camera first, then the event. The whole world is waiting just to get turned into film' (*OTW* 13). Later again, thinking about photography's claim that it 'can show you how the world really is', he realizes that the 'neutral' photographer, 'standing there looking at it is changing the way the world is anyway. If you're going to tell us how things are, then maybe we should start with you' (*OTW* 119). But Harry adds a further (postmodernist) perception:

> Have you noticed how the whole world has changed? It's become this vast display of evidence, this exhibition of recorded data, this continuously running movie.
> The problem is what you don't see. The problem is your field of vision. (A picture of the whole world!) The problem is selection [...] the frame, the separation of the image from the thing. The extraction of the world from the world. (*OTW* 119)

We may notice that the exclamation-mark mockery of the notion of '(A picture of the whole world!)' is cognate with Swift's exposure elsewhere of the impossibility of telling 'the whole story' or 'the whole truth'. In the example Harry gives of this process of 'selection', the photographic media extrapolate and substitute 'an image' of a grenade-throwing marine for the 'real man' who dies seconds after the 'famous shot' was taken: 'the separation of the image from the thing. The extraction of the world from the world.' What is 'postmodern' about this is that it is a striking exemplification of what the simulacrum does and is.

A key event in the present of the novel is the Falklands War: 'A show-case war. An exhibition war', and, pre-empting Jean Baudrillard's view that the Gulf War of 1991 only 'happened' as a media simulacrum,[1] Harry notes that, 'along with the ships and the men, goes a small battalion of camera crews and newsmen' (*OTW* 185), because nowadays 'TV can never have enough "real life" footage. So that it's no longer easy to distinguish the real from the fake, or the world on the screen from the world off it.' Hence, 'it goes without saying that a task force of cameras should accompany the Task Force to the Falklands. As if without them it could not take place' (*OTW* 188–9). And then, crucially, Harry observes: '*the camera no longer recorded but conferred reality*. As if the world wanted to be claimed and possessed by the camera. To translate itself, as if afraid it might otherwise vanish, into the new myth of its own authentic-synthetic memory' (*OTW* 189; emphasis added).

The central and profoundly damaging experience of the postmodern condition, therefore – which the novel proposes in its own postmodernist terms – is that, rather than having its 'myths and legends' dispelled, as the 'recording' camera once seemed capable of doing, 'the world cannot bear to be only what it is. The world always wants another world, a shadow, an echo, a model of itself' (*OTW* 187) – a 'reality' that the photograph in fact 'confers'. In other words, the realist 'story' ('every picture tells a story' (*OTW* 92)) does not protect us from 'myths and legends' (the 'illusion and make-believe' that history teaches us to avoid in *Waterland*), but only offers that fundamental postmodern substitute, the simulacrum. Elsewhere, Harry notes: 'when you put something on record, when you make a simulacrum of it, you have already partly decided you will lose it' (*OTW* 55) – which is why he will not take what Jenny calls 'real photographs' of the Wiltshire countryside or of her own face: 'And I say, "So, if it's beautiful, why photograph it? If you have the reality, who needs the picture?"' (*OTW* 55–6). A photograph – 'the separation of the image from the thing' – is no more than 'an object' that is detached from its material referent: 'it becomes an icon, a totem, a curio. A photo is a piece of reality? A fragment of the truth?' (*OTW* 120). These last phrases, of course, are questions – to which the answers must be at best equivocal. Earlier, and this will return us to Swift's concern with stories and histories, Harry has reflected:

> People want stories. They don't want facts. Even journalists say 'story' when they mean 'event'. Of the news photo they say: Every picture tells a story [...] But supposing it doesn't tell a story? Supposing it shows only unaccomodatable fact? Supposing it shows the point at which the story breaks down. The point at which narrative goes dumb. (*OTW* 92)

Henry James's remark about 'the fatal futility of Fact' seems relevant here,[2] for when a realist 'story' is no more than 'a piece of reality', 'unaccommodatable fact' – seemingly 'real' but no more than a detached image – then 'narrative goes dumb'. However, in the quotation above, there is an implied distinction between kinds of 'story': if people want 'stories' not 'facts', then they want those in which narrative does *not* 'go dumb', and an earlier passing comment of Harry's may give us a clue here: 'photography should be about what you cannot see' (*OTW* 55). In the concluding section of *Out of This World*, which like others of Swift's novels regresses in time to a much earlier period than the chronological present, the 9-year-old Harry finds a sepia photograph of a woman in his father's for once unlocked desk. The woman (it must be his mother) is 'caught' by the photographer in a spontaneous pose: 'Her eyes are wide in happy surprise, her lips are just parted' (*OTW* 204–5). The adult Harry asks:

> Fact or phantom? Truth or mirage? I used to believe [...] that a photo is truth positive, fact incarnate and incontrovertible. And yet: explain to me that glimpse into unreality.
> [...] How can it be that an instant which occurs once and once only, remains permanently visible? How could it be that a woman whom I had never known or seen before – though I had no doubt who she was – could be staring up at me from the brown surface of a piece of paper? (*OTW* 205)

What this seems to suggest is that a photograph that is not just 'unaccomodatable fact', that is 'about what you cannot see' – and, by analogy, a 'story' in which the narrative does not 'go dumb' – can give us a 'glimpse into unreality' that offsets the object-like false 'image' that is merely 'a piece of reality. A fragment of the truth.' True photographs (and 'stories'), in other words, should reveal the real 'unreality' that lies behind the unreal 'reality' (for example, the hidden past, secrets that nevertheless govern people's lives, silences that occlude understanding and intimacy): they should be all about *telling*.

Thus an understated but central theme in *Out of This World*, which goes some way towards controverting both the dominant and factitious 'realism' of news photography and the alienated interpersonal relationships of the characters, is once again – as in *Waterland* – the notion of 'telling (stories)'. We have heard earlier Harry's question to Sophie: 'Someone has to be a witness, someone has to see. And tell? And tell? Tell me, Sophie, can it be a kindness not to tell what you see?' (*OTW* 163). But it is Doctor Klein, Sophie's psychiatrist significantly, who in effect answers the question most succinctly: 'An image, my dear Sophie, is something without knowledge or memory. Do we see the truth or tell it?' (*OTW* 76); and a little earlier, he has glossed 'telling' by commenting: 'the answer to the problem is to learn how to tell. It's telling that reconciles memory and forgetting' (*OTW* 74). Within the novel, the only substantively humanizing moments (of 'kindness') are when characters 'tell' or 'confess' hidden elements of their past to each other. Sophie, of course, is telling 'her-story' to Doctor Klein ('How can I tell, Doctor K? Tell me how to tell it' (*OTW* 109)) – although he too is a detached 'witness' ('Just think of me [...] as two ears and a notebook' (*OTW* 26)), a kind of simulacrum of her father, husband and sons with whom she should be communicating. Reinflecting a question posed explicitly in *Shuttlecock* – and echoing the present novel's epigram ('What the eye sees not, the heart rues not') – she muses: 'What you never know will never hurt you. Is that it? And what you know, you can't ever unknow. Though you can have a damn good try' (*OTW* 26). Here, however, 'unknowing' causes serious breaches in family relationships, and telling and being told seem to hold out the possibility of 'reconciliation'. After all, she is now *telling* Doctor Klein about how she saw her father 'covering' her grandfather's assassination: 'I've never told anyone' (*OTW* 111); she has received a letter from Harry *telling* her about Jenny (*OTW* 98, 140); wants to throw her arms round 'Harry Dad Father' and hug Jenny (*OTW* 145); and is currently on a flight to visit them in England because 'He wants me' (*OTW* 99).

Equally, on the night of the moon landing in 1969, Robert Beech finally '(Sixteen years!)' *tells* Harry that he knew about Anna's affair before she died although not that she was pregnant (*OTW* 168), and asks Harry how *he* knew. Harry – who is in effect also telling Sophie for the first time in his 'confession' to her – replies: 'Because she told me. She – confessed.[...] Before she left she said, "I've got something to tell you." She was crying. She said, "I'm pregnant"' (*OTW* 163–4). A significant exchange then occurs: Robert asks: 'You never thought of telling me?'; Harry counters: '"Why didn't *you* tell *me*?" [...] "All the same, why did you never tell me?"' (*OTW* 169). As the scene ends, Harry does 'that simple but rare thing' and takes his father's (metal) arm, whereupon Robert says: 'I've never told you, have I?' (*OTW* 170–1). Another version of this scene has concluded the opening section of the novel many pages earlier: Robert looks 'as if he, too, didn't know what was real and what wasn't'; Harry says, 'I put my hand on the arm that wasn't his arm.[...] And just a little while after that – it had taken him till he was seventy and I was fifty – he told me how it had happened' (*OTW* 14). Precisely what the father 'told' his son – 'what really happened' when he lost his arm in the First World War after hearing of the death of his wife in childbirth – is never revealed to us. But towards the end of the novel, while Harry is telling Sophie – addressing her directly by name (*OTW* 195) – about her grandfather's story (she has always believed 'He was a hero [...] A real hero' (*OTW* 140)), Harry now says: 'since that night at Hyfield, I have known differently. And I have *never told* anyone. Even when he died and the press were making hay – Death of a Hero [...] I never breathed a word' (*OTW* 196; emphasis added). He suggests that, rather than being a 'real hero', Robert held onto the grenade too long because he was contemplating suicide (*OTW* 197). The 'truth' will never be known ('No camera, of course, was present to record *exactly what happened*' (*OTW* 197; emphasis added) – the irony here is very sharp) because Robert 'himself could not *tell* [...] whether there had been some instant of teetering, agonized indecision' (*OTW* 197; emphasis added). Thereafter, he shut himself away in his munitions work, announcing his retirement to Sophie only the evening before his murder: after 'a fifty-years-and-more *pretence* [...] he was just about to become *a real man* again' (*OTW* 67; emphases added). Sophie has seen a photograph of him before he was wounded when he had 'two *real* arms', and she reflects: 'The strangest thing was the face. The face was alive. Compared to the face of the Grandad I knew [...] the face in the photograph was alive' (*OTW* 62; emphasis added). This is surely another example of photography revealing the 'story' of 'what you cannot see': Robert, the 'real man', before war and the 'arms business' dehumanized him.

The presence of the two sections narrated by Joe and the dead Anna may also be explained by the opportunity it offers for them, too, to 'tell' their 'stories'. Joe's is addressed to a bar-keeper with whom he now spends most evenings as an antidote to Sophie's indifference. Joe 'sell[s] dreams' (*OTW* 153) to Americans in the shape of tours to 'sweet old England' (*OTW* 153), and, Sophie pointedly says, 'is good at forgetting' (*OTW* 42). What his story reveals is, first, that he is himself 'a war baby', and, second, that Sophie's and his passionate youthful love affair is another casualty of the pervasive disease spread by the arms business (Sophie admits: 'I stopped loving him long ago'– in fact, immediately after her grandfather's death (*OTW* 98)). But, while Joe has been writing to Harry and lying to him that 'Sophie's fine', his latest letter admits she 'isn't exactly fine at all' (*OTW* 19): in other words, he is now 'telling' in a way that might lead to reconciliation with Sophie. Will she and the twins return to him? The novel does not say – because they are flying to England in the novel's chronological present. Anna's narrative, on the other hand, delivered from beyond the grave (Swift uses this device again in *Last Orders*), is addressed to 'Dear Harry. Dear husband Harry ...' (*OTW* 173), in which she admits that, until her farewell confession to him about the pregnancy, Frank and she had decided she would have an abortion, 'And say nothing' (*OTW* 180). In the event, she doesn't 'say nothing' but 'tells', and her story here reveals that she was using her affair with Frank as a way of trying to retrieve Harry from the alienating world of war photography: 'It was a tactical affair. A tactical desertion' (*OTW* 174). If this is a tacit confession of her continuing love for Harry from beyond the grave, then the irony is that he will never hear it.

However, it is Harry's 'story' that is central to *Out of This World*, and it is clearly directed to Sophie. That he addresses her in the second person and as 'Sophie' (*OTW* 166, 195) underlines the fact that his narrative is, in effect, one long – and written – confession to her: 'Now look at Harry Beech [...] He is writing a letter. Struggling with words.[...] Dear Sophie. How can I tell you?' (*OTW* 82). But gradually, over the course of the whole book, Harry does 'tell', explaining why he became 'a bad father [...] and a bad son' (*OTW* 22), and how the absence, suppression or loss of love lies at the heart of this. But now, in the novel's present, he is in love again, which has released his ability to 'tell' Sophie 'the truth' about 'what really happened', thus paving the way for reconciliation with her.

But the novel itself, of course, is the overall 'telling': the 'story' that gets behind the 'dumb narrative' of 'unaccommodatable fact' – 'Nothing', says Harry at one point, 'is more cathartic than the conversion of fact into fable' (*OTW* 103). Does the novel's 'telling', however, make it 'true' – or even 'truer' – than the truth-claims of any other kind of realism, photographic or fictional? One effect of the novel's metafictional distantiation of itself from realism (its meditations on photography, for example) is that what it offers us is not 'the truth', but a way of perceiving how notions of the truth are foisted upon us. 'The camera cannot lie' is a fiction, just as is the notion of the 'true' or 'whole' story and of history as a factual record, for there is always another image behind the photograph, another story behind the story, another history behind the history. We construct narratives, as narratives construct us, and historio-graphic metafiction like *Out of This World* shows us how this happens – not least in its own recognition of complicity in the fashioning of 'fables' of 'the truth'.

One last point in confirmation of this complicity: Sophie's Joe specializes in tours to England: 'golden memories of the Old World. Thatched cottages and stately homes. Patchwork scenery. Sweet, green visions' (*OTW* 15). When Sophie is herself flying home, she tells her sons they will 'see all the things [they had] only seen so far in pictures [...] So it will seem that England is really only a toy country. But you mustn't believe that' (*OTW* 192) – just as 'toy guns' are simulacra of 'the real thing'. Sophie knows that Joe has 'the knack [...] of ignoring what he knows and endorsing only the image' (*OTW* 77) – and 'the image', 'without knowledge or memory', we have seen to be a dangerous and deluding 'piece of reality'. The reader knows, however, that 'the image' of a 'toy' England belies the fact that it is on its way to war in the Falkland Islands, that MOD installations lurk in the rural idyll of the countryside, that arms' manufacturers own 'stately homes' and get assassinated. But, equally, the England Harry now inhabits is indeed that of Joe's dream world: 'I was', he says, 'facing up to life in a picture-book cottage' with a 'picture-book façade' (*OTW* 59–60 – a 'façade', of course, may connote a false front or deceiving image) – although he later muses: 'Picture-books aren't real? The fairy-tales all got discredited long ago, didn't they?' (*OTW* 79). It is within this pastoral retreat – 'out of this world' – that he loves Jenny, forty years his junior and 'beautiful. She's incredible. She's out of this world' (*OTW* 36). But for Harry, 'the picture looms before me, exquisitely framed, of building my life round a beautiful girl of twenty-three' (*OTW* 120). Why that threatening word 'looms'? And 'pictures', which necessarily 'frame' things (at once, to shape, to contrive, to delimit, to falsify – as in 'framing someone'), have not had a good press in the novel: 'the image separated from the thing'. In the absolute present of the novel, as we know, Harry is up in a Cessna on a photography trip; and, thinking of his cottage and the pregnant Jenny down below, he 'could almost be guilty of believing [...] the rest of the world doesn't matter. The world revolves round that tinier and tinier figure, as it revolves round a tiny cottage in Wiltshire, where she has taken up residence' (*OTW* 39).

Is this an optimistic, if minimalist, affirmation of love in the grisly twentieth-century world of warfare and simulacra – a beneficent pastoral 'fable' to defeat the 'real' narratives of history? Or does the novel simultaneously sustain and disavow the 'guilty' fantasy of escaping 'out of this world': a pastoral narrative, that is to say, just as specious as any 'true story' offered by photographic news? At one point, Harry says: '[Jenny] makes me feel that the world is never so black with memories [...] that it cannot be re-coloured with the magic paint-box of the heart' (*OTW* 141). Is this a genuine attempt to articulate the return of 'feeling' that love brings to the robotic war photographer, or is the mawkish language here ('the magic paint-box of the heart') a sign of authorial disavowal of Harry's abdication of responsibility for the 'real world'? The novel does not tell us, of course, because it is itself composed of the 'stories' it has constructed and related. How, then, do we get behind those of Harry and Sophie? How, indeed, do we get behind the novel's own constitutive narrative? The short answer is: we don't. All we are left with is a sense of the potency of 'stories' and a suspicion of all narratives claiming to 'record' reality. But equally, without its 'framing' [hi]story – its self-reflexive meditation on the textualization of 'reality'– we would be deprived of the insight the novel provides into how our own knowledge of the world is composed of narratives that purport to be true.

Out of This World, then, like *Waterland*, suggests that 'stories' may be just as (or just as little) truthful as histories or news-stories; that, while 'the conversion of fact into fable' may be 'cathartic', it does not give us 'the whole story'; that the solutions stories offer ('telling' > 'love' > 'reconciliation') are only suspended in the fictional ambience. Should we fail to recognize this, the novel gives us a hefty structural nudge by way of another of Swift's 'telling' titles. In 'the present', both Harry and Sophie are up in aircraft, flying 'above the world' (*OTW* 202); Harry 'know[s] it's *unreal*. Up here in the Cessna', and adds: 'But I don't want to lose her. I don't want to lose her' (*OTW* 189–90; emphasis added); two pages later, Sophie concludes with Joe's last words to her before embarking: 'You mean the world to me' (*OTW* 192); and in her final section (the novel's penultimate one) – where, significantly, she is now addressing her sons – she says of their six-hour plane journey: 'Out of this world! ... Let's just be together, here, above the world.' But she ends with the chilling words: 'And your mother has only six hours' (*OTW* 201–2). We may recall that, in Anna's narrative on her fatal flight to Athens, she thinks: 'I want this journey never to stop. I want to stay up here forever' (*OTW* 181). In *Out of This World*, of course, Harry and Sophie also 'stay up here forever', held in infinite suspension by the limits of the story. But if the story were to continue, would their planes crash – finally causing them to fall 'out of this world', Harry 'losing' Jenny, Sophie no longer able to 'mean the world' to Joe? Or would they land safely, Harry hugging Jenny and then Sophie and the twins? Love? Reconciliation? Happy ever after? The novel does not say – but at least we have the title of Swift's next one: *Ever After*.

4

Ever After

With a title that clearly alludes to a conventional ending for 'telling stories' (and hints ironically at perpetual happiness), Graham Swift's fifth novel is a dense, perhaps over-complex book, but one nevertheless central to his *œuvre* precisely because it attempts to work all his principal concerns simultaneously in one novel. *Ever After* is also a more overtly 'literary' novel than any of the preceding ones, witnessed by the Latin tags scattered throughout, and by the repeated intertextual invocations of Shakespeare's *Hamlet*.

Swift reverts here to a single, first-person, male narrator: 'These are, I should warn you', the novel opens, 'the words of a dead man' (*EA* 1) – well, metaphorically at least. Bill Unwin, in 'the present' of the novel – June/July 1988 – is recovering from a suicide attempt three weeks before at the college where he is a don in an ancient, but unnamed, university situated in the Fens, whose motto, pointedly in the Swift universe, is *Qui quaerit, invenit* (*EA* 175 – 'He who seeks, finds out'). Bill is, as we might now have come to expect, telling the story of ('explaining') how he came to be there and why he swallowed a large number of pills a little while beforehand (in fact, he is *writing it down* (*EA* 4), the significance of which for the novel as a whole will become apparent later). The quasi-scholarly work Bill has been engaged on prior to his failed suicide is editing the notebooks of a nineteenth-century ancestor on his mother's side, Matthew Pearce, who lost his faith during the mid-Victorian furore over evolution. Large parts of this journal, together with Bill's contextualization of and commentary on them, are intercut in the text of Bill's 'story' – and hence also in that of the novel (like Prentis senior's memoirs in *Shuttlecock*). So we do not merely have the chronology of Bill's own life and times to unpack (the novel again cuts backwards and forwards in time), but that of Matthew, too – and the possible relationships there may be between these two 'his-stories'.

Because the two chronologies are so extensive and their intercutting so complex, I will outline them here in tabular form. For both, I will give the year, the event, and then the page number in the text of the novel where the dating reference occurs (or, where necessary, how one can deduce it). Matthew Pearce's first:

1817: Matthew's parents, John – a clockmaker – and Susan, marry (*EA* 94).

1819: Matthew born (*EA* 90).

1830: Matthew's mother dies young (*EA* 95) – a regular occurrence in Swift's fiction).

1841: Matthew (aged 22) leaves Oxford University – where he has developed interests in natural history and geology – to become a surveyor (*EA* 91–3).

1844: Aged 25, Matthew, on holiday in Lyme Bay, Dorset, has a life-changing experience: he sees a fossilized ichthyosaurus at close quarters and 'stare[s] into the eye of a monster' (*EA* 89, 100–3): '... The moment of my unbelief. The beginning of my make-belief ...' (*EA* 101).

4 April 1844 ('April' again): Matthew marries Elizabeth Hunt, the daughter of a country clergyman (*EA* 123), and they are presented with the wedding clock his father has made for them, a clock – bearing the motto *Amor Vincit Omnia* ('Love Conquers All') – that 'has served as a wedding gift over successive generations ever since' (*EA* 45–6).

1847–53: During 'the ten happiest and most fragile years of my life', Matthew and Elizabeth have four children (*EA* 123).

Late 1840s: Matthew meets the Victorian engineer Isambard Kingdom Brunel, while surveying the site for Brunel's Saltash railway bridge (*EA* 130).

1849: The Great Western Railway reaches Plymouth and extends into Cornwall (*EA* 130).

1853/5: Two editions of Charles Lyell's *Elements of Geology* mentioned (they established the great age of the earth).

1854: Matthew's 2-year-old son Felix (Latin for 'happiness'), dies (*EA* 95, 99).

1854–60: Matthew's notebooks begin and end (*EA* 90, 132).

1857: Famous photograph of Brunel (in front of huge steamship chains) mentioned (*EA* 202).

1858: Charles Darwin's *Journal* mentioned by Bill Unwin in 'the present' (*EA* 225).

1859: Publication of Darwin's *Origin of the Species* (*EA* 183) and opening of Brunel's bridge over the Tamar (*EA* 202) mentioned.

June 1860: Matthew's row with Elizabeth's father over faith and evolution (*EA* 179 ff.) – Matthew leaves home and family, and ceases keeping notebooks (*EA* 207).

1862: Elizabeth, 'under new laws', divorces Matthew and marries James Neale, who makes and loses a fortune in copper mining (*EA* 211, 216–17).

12 April 1869 (note month): Matthew's letter to Elizabeth written to accompany the notebooks as he prepares to embark on a ship bound for 'the New World' (*EA* 51–6).

14 April 1869: Matthew perishes at sea when his ship goes down in a storm (*EA* 220).

1872: Matthew and Elizabeth's daughter Lucy marries and receives the clock (*EA* 214) – which is later passed to Sylvia, Bill's mother, on her marriage to his 'father' (more about these scare quotes later) in 1935 (*EA* 33), and thence to Bill on his marriage to his wife, Ruth, in 1959 (*EA* 45).

1906: Elizabeth Pearce, now a widow, dies (*EA* 217).

So what can we take initially from these dates and events in the Pearce family life? First, that the period covers most of the nineteenth century – certainly the Victorian era, and most centrally the acme of mid-Victorian progress and achievement in science and technology, c.1840–70 (Matthew begins his career as a surveyor in 1841 and dies in 1869). Second, that 'his-story' is contextualized with 'real' historical events and personages – especially to do with the great era of engineering (Brunel), geology (Lyell), and evolution theory (Darwin). Third, that Matthew is a child of these times, whose already shaky religious faith, under pressure from geological evidence about the age of the earth and from fossils that point to the process of 'natural selection', is finally destroyed by the death of little Felix ('happiness'), for which, significantly, he 'demand[s] an *explanation, a reason.* Nothing less' (*EA* 127; emphases in original). Matthew is an exemplar, in Tennyson's phrase, of 'honest doubt'[1] metamorphozing into full-blown modern rationalism and scepticism. He represents a key moment in accelerating modernity (leaving Oxford in 1841, he is described as still 'belong[ing] to the Old World. But only just' (*EA* 90)), and in this respect he is, with ironic inflection, truly Bill Unwin's ancestor. Fourth, love and happiness appear to be potential casualties of modern progress (Matthew's crisis of faith alienates Elizabeth well before he leaves her), and the motto on the wedding clock, as we shall see, becomes increasingly ironic as it is handed down the generations. Bill Unwin still has the clock in his 'august Fellow's chambers' in 1988 (*EA* 45), so let us now turn to his chronology:

1890: Colonel Unwin, Bill's 'father', born (he is 'forty-five years old' in 1935, and has fought in the First World War (*EA* 33)).

1911: Sylvia Rawlinson, Bill's mother, born (she is 24 in 1935 (*EA* 33)).

1935: Unwin senior marries Sylvia, a talented singer who has never turned her gift into a career (*EA* 32–3).

December 1936: Bill is born (*EA* 57) in the village of Aldermaston in Berkshire, later to become the home of the British Atomic Weapons Research Establishment (*EA* 197 – we might recognize a familiar Swift trope here).

1939: Sylvia's brother, Jim, is 'killed in the earliest months of the war' (*EA* 34 – and here).

During the Second World War, but before 1945: Bill's 'real' father, a railway-engine driver with whom Sylvia has had an affair in the mid-1930s, is 'killed in the war' (*EA* 158, 200; Bill is only told this shortly before the chronological end of the novel).

5 August 1945: Sylvia and Bill have a birthday tea in Aldermaston, the day before the first atom bomb was dropped on Hiroshima (6 August; Nagasaki on the 9th) and the Second World War ended: 'for *ever after*wards she would share her birthday with the anniversary of the *last pre-atomic day*' (*EA* 229; emphases added).

November 1945: Sylvia and 9-year-old Bill are in post-war Paris where Colonel Unwin is engaged in 'his mysterious present duties' (as with Swift's earlier 'hero-fathers', we never know for certain what these were – but see *May 1988* below), and Sylvia is having a torrid affair with Sam Ellison (his younger brother, Ed, has also been lost at sea in the war (*EA* 35)), an American plastics entrepreneur ten years her junior whose 'goal was ... the polymerization of the world' and who believes passionately in 'substitoots' because 'the real stuff is running out' (*EA* 7).

8 April 1946 (note the month): Colonel Unwin commits suicide in Paris (*EA* 20–1) – whether because he knows about Syvia's affair, because he now knows about Bill's 'true' paternity, or because of his 'mysterious present duties' is never established.

March 1947: Sylvia and Sam marry (*EA* 60).

June 1957: Bill meets Ruth Vaughan, his wife-to-be, at the Blue Moon nightclub in Soho, where she works as a dancer and singer (*EA* 74; later, she becomes a celebrated actress).

August 1957: Bill and Ruth spend their 'first night of bliss' together in a room in the Denmark Hotel, near Paddington Station (once the departure point of the Great Western Railway) (*EA* 257 – see *1849*). This event, characteristically, is the one with which *Ever After* actually ends (*EA* 260–1) – although not by any means is this the end of the novel's full chronology.

1959: Bill and Ruth marry (*EA* 45) – 'When the first Aldermaston marchers set out in the late 1950s [...] We were [...] Too happy, too busy being happy, to worry about the Bomb' (*EA* 249) – although, as we have come to expect in Swift's fiction, they remain childless.

1970: Michael Potter, a professional historian and telly-don at Bill's college, meets his wife-to-be, Katherine, whom he marries in 1972. They, too, remain childless: 'Only the two miscarriages [...] Then nothing' (*EA* 80–2). In 'the present' of the novel, Potter, whose 'special field [is] Victorian idealism and Victorian doubt' (80–1) such that he thinks that *he* should be editing the Matthew Pearce notebooks, is trying to persuade Bill to hand them over to him.

1986: Ruth becomes ill with lung cancer (*EA* 111).

1987: Ruth commits suicide by taking an overdose of drugs (*EA* 111, 115); and Bill's mother, Sylvia, dies of throat cancer (*EA* 25; during her final weeks, she has lost her voice, is in hospital, and has become completely silent – thus joining a growing number of Swift's characters who are silenced in one way or another, especially female ones). Sam endows the Ellison Fellowship at the college where Bill is its first incumbent (*EA* 8, 1).

Early May 1988: Sam tells Bill who his father 'really' was (*EA* 154, 158), and on 19 May, Bill seeks information from a Whitehall department about Colonel Unwin's suicide in 1946 (*EA* 176), later receiving a reply informing him that from the final months of the Second World War, his father 'may have harboured [...] a growing aversion, on conscientious grounds, to the nature of his special duties', these being, 'from the spring of 1945 [...] liaison activities with our wartime allies relating to the development of atomic weapons' (*EA* 192–3).

Late May/early June 1988: Sam dies of a heart attack while copulating with a call-girl in a Frankfurt hotel (*EA* 6).

June 1988: Katherine Potter visits Bill in his college rooms and inexpertly tries to seduce him so that he will release the Pearce notebooks to her husband (*EA* 237 ff.). This fails, and immediately after she has left, Bill swallows the pills in an attempt to kill himself (*EA* 247).

Late June/early July 1988: in the absolute 'present' (his suicide attempt was 'only three weeks ago' (*EA* 4)), Bill is sitting in the college gardens recuperating; the contrite Katherine brings him a picnic lunch; and he suddenly hands her 'no, not these scribbled pages' – i.e. the 'his-story' he is writing (and thus, in effect, the novel we are reading) – 'but a complete, freshly made copy of the Pearce manuscripts.[...] ' "For you," I say. "For both of you. I want you to have it now" ' (*EA* 88). This is the moment at which the novel's linear chronology finally ends – the fact that it concludes chapter 8, when there are twenty-two chapters in the whole novel, merely pointing to Swift's extraordinarily precise but complex narrative trajectory.

Anyone who has followed me so far in earlier chapters will have no trouble in recognizing the key issues and motifs revealed in this chronology: the destructiveness of the Second World War (with the shadow of the First World War behind it) and of its legacy – especially nuclear weapons; the fraught relations between fathers and sons, mothers and sons; historical repetition; the fragility of love; secrets in the past and questions of 'what really happened'; the problematic relationship between truth and falsity, reality and unreality, 'the real thing' and 'substitoots', history and story; and the weaving of all these themes together. What is new, of course, is the insertion into them of the 'his-story' of Matthew Pearce, and we will need to consider later what the significance of this may be. But first let me put a little flesh on the bones of the more familiar issues noted above.

There is little doubt that once again the Second World War is the key formative event of the later twentieth century: almost every character is damaged by it directly or indirectly, but here it is the understated theme of its engendering of atomic weapons that overshadows the post-war world. It is not fortuitous that Bill Unwin's 'father' commits suicide while working to facilitate their development; nor that Bill's engine-driver father 'came from Aldermaston' (*EA* 158), where research into them is carried out; nor that Bill is born in Aldermaston, which became the focus of anti-nuclear protest marches in the late 1950s; nor that he and Sylvia are having tea there the day before the first A-bomb is dropped on Hiroshima – 'the last pre-atomic day' (*EA* 229); nor that, in a telling phrase that relates him to several of Swift's previous 'children of violence', the young Bill, living in Aldermaston, sees himself as 'a child of the future' (*EA* 197) – a child, in other words, of the atomic age and 'fathered' by two men who suffer guilt by association with it. Significantly perhaps, when he and Ruth find 'the real thing' – love ('Ruth and I were the real thing' (*EA* 149) – they are 'too happy [...] to worry about the Bomb' (*EA* 249), but when Bill loses love on Ruth's death, he becomes 'a dead man': 'I think I found the real stuff, the true, real stuff. Now it seems, in this new life, I am turned into plastic. I am born again in plastic' (*EA* 9; he discovers he is 'a plastics heir' on Sam's death (*EA* 7)). And, indeed, the world of the present that Bill inhabits – as usual with Swift, barely sketched in in any detail – is either unreal or in a terminal state: his college's ancient walls [...] have become artificial and implausible, like a painstakingly contrived film set. It is everything beyond that is *real*. If hardly reliable. Out there, we are given to believe [...] the world is falling apart; its social fabric is in tatters, its eco-system is near collapse. *Real*: that is, flimsy, perishing, stricken, doomed. Whereas here ... (EA 2; emphases added)

'Whereas here ...' 'sexy young studs of academe' (*EA* 1) like the childless and philandering Potter offer 'Potter's potted history' to the masses on TV: 'He is, by all accounts, a genuinely accomplished historian. Yet he feels obliged to prostitute himself, for the sake of a little dubious limelight, by turning himself into something he is not' (*EA* 42). Potter, in other words, has become a simulacrum of the 'real' historian. Equally, Bill's college fellowship is endowed by wealth earned from 'sub-stitoots' as part of 'the apotheosis of Sam, a New World clone, into a Real English Gentleman' (*EA* 8), and Bill himself, as its barely qualified incumbent, is regarded as 'an impostor' (*EA* 43). If indeed he has 'turned into plastic', which he regards 'as the epitome of the false' (*EA* 7), then 'maybe it's anteriority [...] I'm looking for. To know who I was' (*EA* 235).

One central question such a search involves is trying to establish who his 'real' father was – as so often in Swift's fiction, easier said than done. 'The fiction of my life' – that 'I am my father's son, meaning my father-whom-I-once-knew-as-my-father's son' (*EA* 160; he adds here, 'I am Hamlet the Dane') – is exploded by Sam (Claudius, the 'substitoot' father) when he tells Bill that his father was 'really' an engine-driver: 'I'm going to tell you, because it's the truth. The truth. And you have to tell the truth, don't you, pal?' (*EA* 157). The problem is that 'the truth' Sam conveys is from an account given him by Sylvia about a 'bust-up' that he did not witness between her and Colonel Unwin when her husband finds out about their affair: 'in the middle of it Sylvie tells him – *and afterwards she tells me she's told him* – that you weren't his son.... And two days later your pa – who isn't your pa, who never was your pa ... he goes and shoots himself' (158; emphasis added). Unfortunately, before her death, Sylvia is immured in silence and cannot 'tell' Bill herself what 'the truth' was – even if she was minded to. This, to repeat a trope I have used in relation to *Waterland*, is the 'hole' in the 'whole story' (Bill implies that he will be giving us 'the full story' early on in the novel (*EA* 8)), and it leads to another hole that Bill as Hamlet equally cannot fill: who or what was responsible for Unwin senior's death? And should he pursue 'vengeance' by killing Claudius/Sam, or kill himself (*EA* 5)? (Actually, Bill reminds me more of Prufrock in T. S. Eliot's poem of 1917, 'The Love Song of J. Alfred Prufrock' ('No! I am not Prince Hamlet, nor was meant to be'), with his endless unanswered questions, self-deprecation, and pathetic fantasies about what *Ever After* repeatedly calls 'romantic love'.)

It is apposite that, the second time Bill refers to his college's motto ('He who seeks, finds out'), he adds: 'I wonder' (*EA* 191). For, as we have heard above, the cause of Colonel Unwin's suicide can never be known for certain: was it 'personal reasons' (*EA* 192: i.e. knowledge of his wife's affair with Sam); was it the discovery that Sylvia's promiscuity meant that he was not Bill's 'real' father; or was it, as the letter from Whitehall suggests, aversion to being involved in the development of nuclear weapons? That same letter reveals that Sylvia was informed of what her husband's secret duties were at the inquiry into his suicide; that she was 'charged to *repeat nothing* of what had been disclosed to her'; and 'that *your mother kept her word*, with commendable compliance, up until her death' (193; emphases added). Sylvia (the 'silent woman'), then, never told Bill what she knew. Framed by the famous lines from Act I, Scene i of *Hamlet* about the disappearance of Hamlet's father's ghost, ' " 'Tis here." – " 'Tis here." " 'Tis gone ..." ', Bill poses a series of similar suppositions about what his mother 'did or didn't know', concluding with one that confirms that *he* will never know 'what really happened':

> That he wasn't my father but she never told him he wasn't my father and invented the *story* of *telling* him he wasn't because it was a) a way of confessing a long-suppressed and burdensome *truth*, and b) it effectively masked ... the *real* cause of his suicide.
> That ...
> That ...   (*EA* 196; emphases added)

Immediately following this, Bill quotes another Latin tag: *Felix qui potuit* ... ('Happy is he who has benefited ...' (the full quotation from Virgil, after the ellipsis, is: 'from reading the causes of things')), and comments: 'I doubt it' (*EA* 196). Hence, 'I do not research my own father. My nameless, engine-driving, killed-in-the-war father', recognizing that it is pointless: 'What difference does it make? The true or the false. This one or that one' (*EA* 204). Instead, Bill grieves for his Unwin father, a man, he now understands, who 'couldn't pretend [...] couldn't turn the blind eye' (*EA* 204–5) – a man of integrity, in other words, like Matthew Pearce, as we shall see, whose 'doubt' is engendered by 'reading the causes of things' and, *pace* Virgil, precisely by the loss of *Felix* ('happiness'). Earlier in the novel, Bill has asked the question about there being no difference between 'the true and the false' in another form: 'So what is real and what is not?' (*EA* 90) – a question that lies at the very heart of *Ever After* and its bleak view of things, in respect of both Bill's 'his-story' and that of Matthew Pearce. The equivocal answer the novel itself seems to give is summed up by a quotation from Act II, Scene ii of *Hamlet* that Bill uses to answer yet another cognate question he poses himself (and us): 'What is the difference between belief and make-believe?'. His 'reply' (Hamlet's, in fact) is: 'For there is nothing either good or bad but thinking makes it so' (*EA* 143). 'What is real and what is not', then, appears to be a matter of whether 'thinking makes it so'. In Swift's novel, this has two principal – and not unexpected – foci: 'love' and 'storytelling'. Let me take the first of these first.

The phrase 'romantic love' is reiterated on many occasions in *Ever After*, usually in relation to Bill and Ruth: 'Romantic love. *A made-up thing*. A concoction of the poets.[...] *Amor vincit omnia*' (111; first emphasis added); 'Romantic love. Romantic love. The first, flustered kiss [...]' – a love terminated only by Ruth's untimely death: 'And in between? Happiness. Yes, I commemorate it. Happiness *ever after*' (121; emphasis added). What Bill and Ruth have is 'the real thing [...] the substance of love' (*EA* 76). Significantly, it is Sam who does not 'understand it, this – romantic love': 'Sam might have admitted that this marriage to my mother was itself a kind of long-term, plausible "substitoot": Ruth and I were the real thing' (*EA* 148–9). But it is Sylvia – 'this woman, so unscrupulous, so indolent, so heartless, my mother' (*EA* 32) – who rubbishes the notion most thoroughly: of the motto on the wedding clock, she tells young Bill, 'It's Latin, darling.[...]"Love conquers all." If only it were true' (*EA* 46).

Well, thinking may make it so, and for Bill this is certainly the case – although whether the novel itself endorses that is another question.

Is Bill, then, a kind of unreliable narrator who fails to see through his own naivety and willingness to believe in 'a made-up thing' ('make-believe')? For Ruth is at once a very determinate absence in the novel (already dead and conveyed to us only in Bill's posthumous adoration) and reputedly a consummate actress. Her mother, early on, had been against 'this play-acting. Don't try to be something you're not ...' (*EA* 114 – thus echoing the phrase about the *faux*-historian Potter who is 'turning himself into something he is not' (*EA* 42)). After Ruth's suicide, Bill is asked by journalists for insights into 'The "real Ruth Vaughan"', but all he can come up with (for us as readers of the novel, too) are vague platitudes: 'How could you describe her face? There was no other word for it: it was full of *life*. So full of life. I think she was beautiful because she was *her*. Because she was Ruth' (*EA* 118; emphases in original). This is as good as saying 'Ruth was Ruth' – which tells us nothing. A little later, however, he makes a revealing remark: 'She represented life to me.[...] She was life to me. And that isn't just vain hyperbole, is it? She was an actress, wasn't she? It was her job to represent life to people' (*EA* 120). As we read the first sentence here, we tend to take the phrase 'represented life to me' in the more colloquial sense that she seemed to be the epitome of life ('was life to me'), but when the phrase is repeated in the final sentence, it has mutated into the sense of representation as *artifice* – in Ruth's case, as *acting*. In other words, she produces a very convincing simulacrum of 'the real thing' ('life'), but is not 'the real thing' itself – indeed we might say, given her cancer and the fact that she takes her own life, that she is death masquerading *as* life. Late on in the novel, this trope of acting and death is reinforced when Bill remembers looking at her corpse and wanting her to come back as 'a person': 'I wanted to say, just like people do in cheap dramas: "Don't! Please! Come back!" I wanted to say – as if it really were some (convincing) death scene – "Ruth, stop acting! Please. Stop acting"' (*EA* 235–6). And very much earlier, he confirms how difficult it was to know or possess 'the real Ruth Vaughan':

I would watch her disappear and turn into – these other people. With my own eyes I witnessed the *inconstancy*. How many times did I watch Ruth fall into another man's embrace?[...] How many times did I watch her – die? And [...] I would have to concede that at such moments she didn't belong to me, she belonged to her audiences. She was everybody's. But the thing is, she would always come back to me. (*EA* 111; emphasis added)

The question one poses here is: what did this 'inconstant' being come back to Bill *as*: 'the real Ruth Vaughan' or merely a representation of herself, playing yet another part? And if she only 'represents life' to Bill, then what of 'romantic love'? Is this no more than a 'representation', a simulacrum of 'the real thing', too – a fantasy in his Prufrock-like 'Love Song' to her memory. Once again thinking about the onset of her illness and her death, he says: 'Her last role was Cleopatra. Love triumphant and transcendent. Love beyond the grave' (*EA* 111). What the novel seems to imply is that 'romantic love' in 'real life' – certainly in the sense implied by 'they lived happily *ever after*' – is a delusion, although importantly one that as 'make-believe', 'a made-up thing', 'a concoction of the poets' – a 'story' even? – may help us to navigate life in 'the real world'. Rightly or wrongly, Bill 'still believe[s] in' 'Literature' (*EA* 5): 'There has always been, for me, this other world [...] to fall back on – a more reliable world in so far as it does not hide that its premise is illusion. Even when I left it to enter – what? the real world? the theatre? – I made sure [of] a good stock of that other world' (*EA* 69). 'Romantic love' and 'happiness' may be possible in that 'other world', which 'does not hide that its premiss is illusion' (unlike 'the real world'), and it is here that we may segue across to that other focus of *Ever After* where 'thinking makes it so': 'telling stories'.

Large portions of Matthew Pearce's notebooks are 'reproduced' in the text of the novel – and a very convincing pastiche of a Victorian journal Swift has produced (for it is as well to remember that this is 'a made-up thing', too). But beyond these excerpts, Bill himself also adds extensively to Matthew's story of love, happiness, doubt and disaster. In this context, we may register the verb forms Bill constantly uses in his narrative; for example: 'He *would have* understood [...]'; 'It *would be* like him [...]'; 'And it *must have* dawned on him [...]' (*EA* 95–7 and *passim*, chapter 9). What these conditional forms tell us is that Bill is *speculating* about Matthew – suggesting things the notebooks do not contain and that Bill could never really know. This is confirmed by more overt 'authorial' intrusions in the same chapter: 'I see him (I have no proof of this; I have no idea what he looked like at all) [...]' (*EA* 91); 'What he will not be aware of [...]' (*EA* 96); 'You have to imagine these scenes [...]' (*EA* 101); 'No one will ever know how he is not himself [...] And the only remedy he has is to pretend'; 'Or that is how I like to see it. That is how I wish it to have happened' (*EA* 103). Finally, Bill comes clean: 'I invent all this. I don't know that this is *how it happened*' (*EA* 109; emphasis added); and later he says: 'What do I know of Matthew? I conjure him up, I invent him.[...] I drag him into the light' (*EA* 145). It is not fortuitous that, in Bill's college's motto, the Latin word *invenit* ('finds out') derives from the same root as the word that gives us 'invent': *invenio, inveni, inventum*. So that what the motto *can* mean is: 'He who seeks, *invents* it' – or better, perhaps, 'makes it up'. And that is exactly what Bill is doing with the Matthew Pearce 'story': 'thinking makes it so'.

Earlier in chapter 9 occurs a crucial passage in understanding what *Ever After* is about. Bill is reflecting on his method of editing the Pearce notebooks:

> The facts infused with a good deal of theory, not to say imagination.[...] The facts, mixed with a good deal of *not necessarily false invention*.[...] I am not in the business of *strict historiography*. It is a prodigious, presumptuous task: to take the skeletal remains of a single life and attempt to breathe into them their former *actuality*.[...] As Ruth would have said, the script is only a beginning: there is the *whole life* [emphasis in original]. Let Matthew be *my creation*.[...] And if I *conjure* out of the Notebooks a complete yet hybrid being, *part truth, part fiction, is that so false*? I only concur, surely, with the mind of the man himself, who must have asked, many a time: So what is real and what is not? (90; emphases added)

Notice here the opposition between 'facts' and 'fiction', 'strict historiography' and 'not necessarily false invention'; the suggestion that what is 'made up' ('my creation') may be as, if not more, 'truthful' than a 'factual' account; and that familiar question at the end in relation to all this: 'So what is real and what is not?' In other words, Bill's 'story', 'a little bit of creative licence? A little bit of fiction?', may get closer to the truth than

'some vapid period piece [...] [like] Potter's TV "realization"'
(*EA* 185) – or indeed any professional historian's edition of the
notebooks, with all its scholarly apparatus and contextualization
in 'Victorian idealism and Victorian doubt' (*EA* 80–1). But how
may we relate this promotion of 'make-believe' to our other
focus: 'romantic love'? Quite simply because Bill wants Matthew
and Elizabeth to be happy: 'I invent. I imagine. I want them to
have been happy. How do I know they were ever happy? I
make them fall in love at the very first meeting on a day full of
radiant sunshine. How do I know it was ever like that?' (*EA* 212).
The pat answer is: because 'thinking makes it so', but notice, too,
the tense of verb Bill uses: 'to *have been* happy'. Even he cannot
prevent the extinction of happiness (after all, 'Felix' dies,
Matthew loses his faith, and his marriage falls apart): even Bill
cannot invent an 'ever after'. Nevertheless, he has a jolly good
try; for late on in his story, speculating about why Elizabeth held
onto Matthew's notebooks and his accompanying letter (if she
hadn't, they would never have come down into Bill's posses-
sion), he wonders: 'did she stop loving him, as (so she believed,
let's suppose) he had stopped loving her? Or did she love him
still [...]?' (*EA* 219). The equivocal parenthesis there – 'let's
suppose' – is crucial to the answer Bill this time gives to his own
question: 'He loved her. He wrote it down: that flimsy, romantic
thing, a love-letter. And Elizabeth? She kept the letter, she kept
the Notebooks. She loved him still' (*EA* 221). Like that of Bill and
Ruth, this is 'Love triumphant and transcendent. Love beyond
the grave' (*EA* 111), and that, it seems – combined with *Ever
After*'s other two 'endings': Ruth and Bill in 1957 (final pages);
Bill giving Katherine the Pearce Notebooks in 1988 (end of
chapter 8) – is the limit of the novel's ability to make an
affirmation. I am reminded here of E. M. Forster's 'Terminal
Note' to his posthumously published homosexual novel,
Maurice, in which he says: 'A happy ending was imperative.[...]
I was determined that in fiction anyway two men should fall in
love and remain in it for the ever and ever that fiction allows'.[2]

'The ever and ever that fiction allows': thus we may note that,
in the Pearce ending quoted above, love also survives because it
is 'written down': 'that flimsy, romantic thing, a love-letter' –
which is significantly 'reproduced' in its entirety as chapter 5 of
Swift's novel. And Bill, of course, is writing 'his-story', too,

which includes Matthew's (and thus comprises *Ever After* as 'the full story'): 'Part fact and part surmise, just like my reconstruction of the life of Matthew Pearce. Just [...] like my reassembly, here in this afterworld, of my own life' (*EA* 80). Since 'the past, they say, is a foreign country', all Bill can do 'is fictionalize (perhaps) these memories' (*EA* 229 – note the equivocating parenthesis again). Late on, as a 'dead man', he registers 'a strange, concomitant yen, never felt before, to set pen to paper.[...] To [...] write a book. The struggle for existence? Ha! The struggle for *remembrance*' (231; emphasis in original). But just before the end of Bill's story and of the novel – in which, we will recall, he is remembering that 'first night of bliss' with Ruth and the expectation that they will live happily ever after – he makes a crucial, if finally unspoken, distinction between himself and Matthew. He says: 'I would believe or not believe anything, swallow any old make-believe, in order to have Ruth back. Whereas Matthew—— Whereas this Pearce guy——' (*EA* 256). How do we complete these sentences? Perhaps by adding: 'Whereas this Pearce guy faced the truth, distinguished between "belief and make-belief", stared the monstrous "real thing" in the eye.'

For the point, I think, of the insertion of Matthew's story into Bill's contemporary one is to make a comparison between Victorian doubt and late-twentieth-century anomie – the one rigorous, finally unflinching, honest, marked by integrity; the other flabby, equivocating, self-deceiving, a 'substitoot' for 'the real thing'. When Potter, trying to cajole Bill into releasing the notebooks to him, says: 'The spiritual crisis of the mid-nineteenth century is *my subject*', Bill thinks: 'Uttered in the late twentieth century [...] these words, if they had not carried such urgency, would have had a comic splendour' (*EA* 164; emphasis in original). In his farewell letter to Elizabeth, Matthew writes 'that though ignorance may be bliss, happiness is not purchased by refusal of knowledge. Where there is evidence, so we must look, so we must examine' (*EA* 52). This might be an early forebear of Tom Crick in *Waterland* preaching the continual need for the question 'Why?', for 'curiosity', for 'explanation'. If the modern world will 'swallow any old make-believe' in the pursuit of an illusory 'romantic love', Matthew recognizes that 'happiness is not to be purchased by a refusal of knowledge'. For ten years, from first seeing the ichthyosaurus and before the death of Felix, Matthew has 'pretended' that his faith is not in question: '... The moment of my unbelief. The beginning of my make-belief ...' (EA 99, 101) – so that his notebooks are what Bill later calls 'a record of his life as a fiction. From now on [i.e. Matthew having come clean to his family in 1860 when the notebooks finish], he would be "real" – he would live according to how things truly were' (EA 183). Knowledge, however, will not necessarily bring happiness either – it will not bring back Felix – but it has to be faced, even when it totally undercuts one's whole life. In the same letter to Elizabeth, Matthew states: 'There has been no counter-reversal, no retracting of retraction. I hold to my groundless ground' (EA 55). It is his ability to 'hold to groundless ground' (one thinks of the unstable reclaimed land in Waterland), to 'live according to how things truly were', that is Matthew's (and the Victorians') great quality – one that Bill as late-twentieth-century man so signally lacks.

Finally, we might want to ask why Bill, in the absolute present of the novel, hands over to Katherine Potter 'a complete, freshly made copy of the Pearce manuscripts' for her historian husband to edit and contextualize as a fine example of 'the spiritual crisis of the mid-nineteenth century'. Note, however, that all Potter will receive is 'a freshly made copy', another 'substitoot', but only of 'unaccommodatable fact', as Out of This World has it, in which 'narrative goes dumb'. Bill's gift is partly an attempt by this proponent of 'romantic love' to rescue the Potters' marriage ('And children? Children can be adopted. Substitutes can be arranged' (EA 246; emphasis added). But surely more pointedly, 'these scribbled pages', which Bill shuffles into his briefcase out of Katherine's sight before giving her the 'copy' of the notebooks, are paradoxically 'the real thing' in which 'dumb' narrative is made to speak, pages that already contain the true 'story' of both Matthew Pearce and Bill Unwin – 'a little bit of fiction' of 'not necessarily false invention' that charts the spiritual crisis of the mid-nineteenth century but also the spiritual malaise of the late-twentieth century. Story outwits and displaces history once more – for 'these scribbled pages' are, of course, Swift's novel.

5

<hr>

Last Orders

Swift's sixth novel won the Booker Prize for fiction in 1996, and is, as we shall see, a more subtly 'literary' novel than *Ever After*, whilst it reworks many of his established themes in new ways. The focus is much narrower and tighter in *Last Orders*, both spatially and temporally, the setting being largely restricted to south-east London and its Kent hinterland, and the action to one day in the present – 2 April 1990[1] (note the month especially here) – although a past chronology (more compressed than hitherto) is introduced by flashbacks in the minds of the principal characters, and is, not unexpectedly, of central significance to the novel's overall project. This chronological structure is as precise and covert as usual – often requiring careful deductive reading to establish some of its principal dates – and, once again, the novel acts as a kind of historical explanation for the current circumstances of its characters: how the past is the matrix of the present.

Formally more like *Out of This World* than any other of Swift's fiction to date, *Last Orders* is composed of multiple short sections, with abrupt headings that indicate either a place (for example, 'Bermondsey', 'Gravesend', 'Rochester') or the name of the character mentally 'narrating' the section in question. For this time the novel is mainly told – in a brave but convincing piece of ventriloquism on Swift's part – through the south London voices of four men: Ray Johnson, insurance clerk (nicknamed 'Lucky' for escaping the Second World War unscathed and for his prowess at betting); Lenny 'Gunner' Tate, ex-Second World War artilleryman, ex-boxer and fruit-and-veg trader; Vic Tucker, ex-Second World War seaman, now an undertaker; and Vince Dodds, Second World War orphan, now a car salesman. On 2 April 1990 they are being driven by Vince down to Margate on the Kent coast to cast into the sea the ashes of their dead friend, Jack Dodds, also a Second World War veteran and an ex-butcher (like Anna in *Out of This World*, he narrates one section from 'the other side'). That this event should be happening is the consequence of his 'last orders' to his wife, Amy, who will not go on the trip herself but persuades Ray and his friends to fulfil Jack's wishes, and who is given six sections to narrate (mainly addressed to her brain-damaged daughter, June). Mandy, Vince's wife, the only other 'voice' in the novel, also narrates one section; otherwise, the novel comprises the 'his-stories' of the four living men. It is worth adding, though, that the 'place' sections are in fact narrated by Ray – as is made clear on the first page of the first section, 'Bermondsey': 'He frowns [...] looking at me. "Course, Ray", he says and moves off down the bar' (*LO* 1).

Chronologically, the first important implied 'event' (it is never quite narrated) is the coupling of Jack and Amy in late August 1938 while hop-picking at Wick's Farm in Kent (*LO* 234–8), the result of which is their severely retarded daughter, June, who is born on 1 June 1939 (*LO* 83) and who, for all her fifty years in 'a home for the hopeless' (*LO* 239), never speaks a word (*LO* 173) – thus becoming yet another of Swift's institutionalized silent (women) characters. During the summer of 1939, Jack and Amy spend a honeymoon weekend in Margate, but Amy already knows that Jack is becoming alienated from her because of June: 'it was only after you arrived that I felt him tug away [...] and turn against me [...] as if it was really all my fault now, my problem, not his' (*LO* 238). In fact, Jack's attitude to June is summed up in the sentence: '*Best thing we can do, Ame, is forget all about her*' (*LO* 253), and this is effectively what he does for the next fifty years, never visiting her in 'the Home' (*LO* 171) – 'His own flesh and blood' (*LO* 85) – while Amy visits her twice every week without fail (*LO* 169). During the Margate weekend, in a shooting booth at the end of the pier, Jack wins a prize and Amy chooses a teddy bear, which Jack proceeds to throw into the sea – the significance of which action will become clear later on.

The reader will already have noticed that the above events take place on the brink of the Second World War in September 1939 – and war is once again a determinate factor in shaping the lives of all the novel's main characters. Amy hopes that 'the war might change things' vis-à-vis her, Jack and June, 'But what the war did was to push things further the way they'd gone. It was you and me together [...] and Jack far away being a soldier' (*LO* 239). And indeed Jack and Ray are on active service in North Africa in 1942 fighting at 'the battle of El Alamein' (*LO* 100; 'A small man at big history', says Ray of himself (*LO* 90)), while 'somewhere in the same desert, Lenny Tate was advancing and retreating' (*LO* 90). A vestigial sense of the war's persistence into the present is flagged when Ray exclaims to Lenny that Vince's car is ' "A Merc." Lenny says, it's like a joke he's been saving up for fifty years, "Rommel *would* be pleased" ' (*LO* 12). Vic spends the war in the navy, where, because of his family's undertaking business, he is put in charge of preparing the dead for burial at sea (*LO* 123–6). But another thing 'the war did' was to kill Vince's birth parents when he was only a few months old, their home being destroyed by a 'doodlebug' (German flying bomb) in June 1944 (*LO* 42). Amy takes Vince in and he is adopted by her and Jack, although 'I ought to have known [...] it wouldn't win [Jack] back. You can't make a *real thing* out of pretending hard' (*LO* 240; emphasis added). So here we are again: Vince, a 'substitoot' son for Jack who cannot accept him as the 'real thing', while Vince himself thinks: 'It's like I'm not real, I aint ever been real' (*LO* 35). We may take it, then, that Vince, who pointedly describes himself as 'son of a doodlebug' (*LO* 103), is yet another damaged 'child of war', with the father–son relationship always 'at daggers drawn' (*LO* 240), and Vince refusing to join the family butchery business of 'Dodds and Son'. It is no surprise, therefore, that in 1962, having got Lenny's daughter, Sally, pregnant (*LO* 44–5), Vince signs up in the army for five years and does a tour in the Middle East (*LO* 44), being demobbed in 1967.

In the winter of 1965, Ray's daughter, Susie, leaves with her Australian boyfriend for Sydney (*LO* 55, 57), never to return, and soon afterwards Ray stops writing to her, so that in 1990 father and daughter have been out of contact 'for nigh on twenty-five years' (*LO* 282), although, in his 'present' narrative, Ray is mentally addressing Susie – like Harry's 'confession' to Sophie in *Out of This World*. In April 1966 (note the month), he buys a camper van, whereupon his wife Carol leaves him for another man (*LO* 59–60). Ray begins to take Amy Dodds in the van on her Thursday visits to see June (*LO* 169–73), and in 1967 ('It was a bright, breezy day in April'), Ray and Amy start an affair that lasts fourteen weeks (*LO* 174–5), ending it only when Vince is demobbed – 'fresh back from the arse-hole of Arabia' (*LO* 103) – and Mandy arrives at the Dodds' home in London from Blackburn (*LO* 153). The choice of the year 1967 is a good example of Swift's minimalist 'real' contextualization of his fictional stories, for it is both 'The year of Sergeant Pepper. Four thousand holes in Blackburn, Lancashire' (*LO* 158) and the year Britain finally evacuated its armed forces from Aden (Vince is 'one of the last troops to clear out of Aden' (*LO* 69)), thus indicating that it was abandoning any role east of Suez and was effectively no longer a world power. Thereafter, Vince sets up a car dealership, buying Ray's scrapyard off him dirt cheap in 1968 (*LO* 248), marries Mandy around 1970, has a daughter, Kath, who is 18 in 1988 and who Vince uses as bait to sell an Arab client a car, thinking: 'There goes Vince Dodds who pimps for his own daughter' (*LO* 166, 168).

Vince's fortieth birthday is in 1984, when it is also the 'hundredth' (*LO* 6) of the Coach and Horses pub in Bermondsey, where the main characters meet on the morning of 2 April 1990 before setting off for Margate. This gives rise to 'Ray's joke' that '"It aint never gone nowhere [...] Daft name to call a pub.[...] When it aint ever moved"' (*LO* 6–7). And, as 'last orders' are called (*LO* 9), Ray repeats his joke – 'But it aint ever gone nowhere, has it?' – to which Jack replies: 'Where d'you think it should be going, Raysy? Where d'you think we've all got to get to that the bleeding coach should be taking us?' (*LO* 9). The answer, perhaps, is down to Margate in a casket. June is 50 on 1 June 1989 (*LO* 83), and, while Amy is visiting her as usual, Jack tells Vic: 'Moment's come [...] I'm going to sell up the shop' (*LO* 81). He plans 'a new life' for himself and Amy in a bungalow down in Margate, but Amy muses: 'As if we could put the clock back and start off again where it all stopped. Second honeymoon. As if Margate was another word for magic' (*LO* 229). Within months, however, Jack 'goes down with a nasty touch of stomach cancer' (*LO* 14) and dies in March 1990. But just before doing so – 'no new life, eh? Not for me' (*LO* 221) – he borrows £1,000 off Vince and asks Ray to put it on a horse for him, because five years earlier he had taken out a loan to save the shop, which is now due for repayment and would cripple Amy. Ray places the bet on a rank outsider at thirty-three to one, and wins; later, he asks Amy: ' "What was he doing at the end?" Amy said, "He was sitting up in bed listening to the radio, and then [...] he took off his headphones, all neat and careful, and said, 'That's it then. That's all right then,' [...] and when [the nurse] came back he was dead" ' (LO 293). Jack has 'come to terms. It's Amy I'm thinking of' (LO 220) – or, as Lenny puts it elsewhere, 'It's a question of paying your dues' (LO 132).

And that, too, is what Jack's four friends are doing on 2 April 1990 as they drive down to Margate to fulfil his 'last orders'. Despite being interspersed with fragments of 'his-stories', and the continual intercutting of mental flashbacks within the individual sections, Last Orders, unlike Swift's earlier novels, retains a linear narrative structure as far as the progress of the day is concerned. So that the men meet at the Bermondsey pub in the morning in the first section of the novel, then drive down the Old Kent Road – significantly passing a pub called the 'Thomas à Becket' on the way (LO 17; see below, p. 87) – cross Blackheath and motor on into Kent, have a boozy lunch in Rochester, and then, on Vic's request, visit the memorial to the dead of two world wars above Chatham: 'All These Were Honoured in their Generation and were the Glory of their Times' (LO 129), but of which Ray pointedly remarks: 'It's like it got built then forgotten' (LO 122) – twentieth-century wars are regularly and dangerously subject to 'forgetting' in Swift's work. They decide to take 'Jack' to visit Canterbury Cathedral, and as they arrive, Ray muses, 'It's like we aren't the same people who left Bermondsey this morning, four blokes on a special delivery. It's like somewhere along the line we just became travellers' (LO 193–4) – or, one might suggest, pilgrims. In the Cathedral, Lenny reckons Vince is 'trying to make amends', adding: 'We've all got a bit of that to do if you look back over the years', immediately also thinking of his daughter, Sally, whose abortion he had forced upon her – 'And she aint ever forgiven me since' (LO 203–4) – and wondering if he should 'go and pay [her] a visit' (LO 209). Likewise, Ray is thinking that with the money he's won he could fly to Australia and be reconciled with his daughter, Sue. After Canterbury, they finally reach Margate and achieve their mission, each throwing handfuls of ashes into the sea. And so the novel's chronology comes full circle: from 1939 when Jack throws the teddy bear off the end of the Pier to 1990 when Ray, Lenny, Vic and Vince throw 'Jack' off the end of the Pier too.

What may be gleaned from all this regarding the main themes in *Last Orders*? First, clearly, the Second World War continues to exert a malign influence over the wasted lives of its characters, all of whom seem trapped in the stasis of their damaged interpersonal relations – between husbands and wives, and between parents (especially fathers) and children (especially daughters). One telling comment in this context is made by Vince to Mandy: 'If it weren't for Hitler, Jack would never've budged from that shop' (*LO* 105). But the war only alienates him further from Amy, and in fact Jack never does 'budge from that shop': in Amy's words, 'I watched him set solid into Jack Dodds the butcher' (*LO* 229). At one point, Vince taunts Jack: 'Your own man? You never were your own man. You were your old man's man, weren't you?' (*LO* 24), for it transpires that what Jack really wanted to be was a doctor not a butcher, but 'the old man wouldn't have it otherwise. Dodds and Son [...]' (*LO* 27). Equally, Amy knows that she herself is 'stuck in a mould of my own. Of the woman who sits every Monday and Thursday afternoon on a number 44 bus' (*LO* 229). Because she 'chooses' June, and therefore effectively rejects Jack, she imprisons herself in June's non-life: 'That's what I am, that's what I've been: a visitor' (*LO* 274), and she scoffs at Jack's idea that 'we're going to be new people' (*LO* 15). Ray, too, sees Jack and Amy's life as having been 'put in a mould long ago and come out solid', but he also adds: 'I suppose we all do that' (*LO* 170–1). So that Ray – whose estranged wife and daughter have long since left him – also thinks to himself: 'it aint living you're doing, they call it living, it's surviving' (*LO* 128). And then there is Lenny, who forced his daughter to have a botched abortion so that she can no longer have children (*LO* 208, 70), and after a failed marriage starts 'having visitors of her own, paying guests. It's a living, you can see what drives a woman to it' (*LO* 276). Like Lenny, Vince is also the cause of his daughter prostituting herself ('a daughter on the hustle', says Mandy (*LO* 161)). Vic alone seems to be undamaged (Ray thinks: 'I reckon Vic's got it all sorted out' (*LO* 284)). His sons have joined the family business ('*Tucker and Sons*' (*LO* 47)), as he did before them, but when Jack asks him: 'Boys okay, Vic?',

Vic thinks: 'Boys, they're both over forty. But it's what I call them: boys' (*LO* 83). So he and they, too, are imprisoned in a kind of time warp. A little earlier, reflecting on his 'trade', Vic muses: 'You have to be raised to it, father to son. It runs in a family, *like death itself* runs in the human race, and there's comfort in that. *The passing on*' (*LO* 78; emphases added). Hence Vic's trade, even though 'a good trade, a steady trade. It won't ever run short of custom' (*LO* 78), is itself a form of death-in-life – 'The passing on' – which enfolds both himself and his 40-year-old 'boys'.

All these lives, therefore – in which love once again has been destroyed and is now conspicuous only by its absence – 'aint never gone nowhere', to pick up Ray's joke about the Coach and Horses: except towards death, as Jack's response to the joke implies (*LO* 7, 9). And it is Jack's single, short and enigmatic section from beyond the grave, towards the end of *Last Orders*, that acts as a gloss on all this. Significantly, it is made up entirely of advice from his father – ostensibly about the butcher's trade: 'Jack *boy* [note the form of address], it's all down to wastage.[...] You got to keep a constant eye on wastage, constant. What you've got to understand is the nature of the goods. Which is perishable' (*LO* 285) – and there the section ends. Human lives, it seems to say, are 'perishable' and extremely susceptible to 'wastage' – as witnessed by the lives of all the characters here. On several occasions in the later pages of the novel, Ray and Amy refer to 'Dreamland' (in Margate): Amy, thinking about the failed relationships in her life, says ruefully: 'Let's all go to Dreamland' (*LO* 276), and Ray describes Margate's seaside attractions thus:

> They're all painted up and decked out like poor men's palaces, except one [...] looming over them all, a bare brick tower with just a few big words on it. It looks more like the way into a prison than a funfair.[...] It's what Margate's famous for, it's what people come here for. *Dreamland*. (*LO* 273)

If we combine the notion of 'wastage' with the notion of 'Dreamland', we may come up with: 'Wasteland' – as both an all-encompassing term for the dereliction of the novel's post-war 'wasted' lives, and, as I hope to make clear below, a significant and extended allusion to T. S. Eliot's poem of that title.

83

But before I do so, it is worth registering – as in all Swift's fiction – that these wasted lives are full of 'secrets', of pieces of knowledge that the owners have never told about – except, of course, in the 'stories' they are now 'telling' in the confessional narratives that comprise the novel. As Amy says of the night June was conceived: 'Jack won't ever know it was the sight of that gypsy. The things that do and don't get told' (*LO* 240). That these 'stories' are often mentally addressed to those with whom the narrators most want a reconciliation we will see later is a central feature of an unexpectedly positive – if still equivocal – theme in *Last Orders*. At the end of the section where Vic describes seeing Ray and Amy together during their affair in 1967, he says: 'What you learn in this business is to keep a secret' (*LO* 219), so that when Jack announces to him in 1989 that he's decided to quit his shop, Vic asks 'You sure you're going to tell Amy? I'm your witness now, Jack', and thinks to himself: 'I'm a witness, all right. Shall I tell him?' (*LO* 85). But he never does. Likewise Amy with the dying Jack: 'he doesn't say, "And give June my love." So I think, Then I won't mention Ray, I won't say a thing about Ray.[...] Fair dos. What you don't know can't hurt' (*LO* 268). There again is that ambiguous Swiftian phrase, and we are left uncertain, from a couple of sly things Jack says on his deathbed to Ray ('So now I know, Raysy.[...] No telling is there?' (*LO* 152)), as to whether he knew or not about what went on in the camper van, just as Ray is never sure whether Vince, too, had his suspicions: 'And now I think that [...] he never knew then and he doesn't know now either. Because he'd've said, by now, he'd've come right out with it, today of all days' (*LO* 251). When Vince lends Jack £1,000 before he dies, he says: 'I'm not telling no one [...] about Jack's little last request' (*LO* 23), just as Jack refuses to reveal to Ray where he got the money: 'Be telling, wouldn't it?' (*LO* 224). And when Ray learns from another man of Jack's thwarted ambition to become a doctor, the friend says: ' "You won't tell Jack" [...] "No" I say, sort of thoughtful, as if I might.[...] But I never did tell Jack, and Jack never told me' (*LO* 27–8). Of the photograph on the Dodds' sideboard of Jack and Ray on a camel in Egypt in 1942, Ray thinks: 'And Amy never knew, and she still don't, what we were doing just hours before that photo was taken': that they were in a Cairo brothel. When Jack informs Ray about the loan he needs to repay before he dies, Ray asks him: ' "You told Amy about all this?" He shakes his head. I say, "You going to?" [...] He says, "Some things are best not known" ' (*LO* 222–3), and we wonder again what he is referring to. Equally, no one knows about Ray's final bet for Jack, and Ray is in two minds, right up to the end of the novel, about whether to confess to Vince about his winnings ('Jack aint going to tell no one' (*LO* 200)) or Amy about her windfall (but see below, p.90). And it takes Ray twenty-five years to admit to his daughter how and when his wife Carol deserted him: 'I thought not writing at all was better than thinking up lies' (*LO* 281). But now, in the present and about to 'pay his dues' to Jack, he imagines going to Australia to visit her: 'But here I am anyway, now, *telling you*, saying it to your face.[...] And the fact is I stopped missing [Carol] a long time ago [...] but I aint never stopped missing you' (*LO* 282; emphasis added). Ray's 'telling' and 'confession' of his feelings for Susie are a form of expiation, which *Last Orders*, unlike Swift's other fiction up to this point, brings to centre stage.

It is here that we might usefully consider the major literary allusions that help to structure the novel, thence returning to whatever possibilities for redemption it may proffer. When *Last Orders* won the Booker Prize in 1996, one critic pointed out close similarities between it and William Faulkner's early classic novel of American modernism, *As I Lay Dying* (1930), implicitly accusing Swift of plagiarism and causing a media row.[2] The *donnée* in both novels is indeed much the same – in *As I Lay Dying* the body of their dead mother is being transported on a cart by members of her family for burial in a Southern town some 40 miles away in order to fulfil her last wishes – and there are close structural similarities, too. Each section of Faulkner's novel is headed solely by the name of one of the characters, as in *Last Orders*, and contains his or her 'stream of consciousness'; each novel includes a section narrated by the dead person; a single-page section of *As I Lay Dying* is a numbered list of the techniques used by Cash to make his mother's coffin, while in *Last Orders* there is a half-page section entitled 'Ray's Rules', which also gives a numbered list of the principles on which Ray bases his betting (*LO* 202; it ends: '8. You can blow all the rules if you're Lucky'); both novels have a complete section less than five words long (Swift's is Vince thinking: 'Old buggers' (*LO*

130)). However, leaving aside the improbable likelihood that an established contemporary novelist would plagiarize a well-known modernist text and expect to get away with it, *Last Orders* uses its named sections to quite different effect – principally to reinvoke the past – while *As I Lay Dying* concerns itself almost exclusively with the present and the immediate mental processes of its characters. A more credible explanation of Swift's 'imitation' of the earlier novel (during the row, he himself referred to it as 'an echo' and an 'allusion'[3]) is that it is a kind of literary joke, as Ray's final deflationary 'rule' and Vince's 'chapter' cited above would suggest. The novel seems to me to be a playful version of 're-visionary' writing, in which a canonic text from the past is reworked by a modern writer for more or less serious purposes and becomes an intertextual 'shadow' for the new work. *Last Orders* seems to ask: what happens to Faulkner's solemn representation of the mentality of Southern whites in early twentieth-century USA when it is transposed into the demotic discourse of a bunch of late-twentieth-century south Londoners? And, at a more serious level, it may point to the possible limitations of *As I Lay Dying* – largely enclosed in the present thoughts of its characters and suggesting little significance beyond them.

Of far greater intertextual interest, however, is the way Swift's novel subtly alludes throughout to T. S. Eliot's equally classic modernist poem, *The Waste Land* (1922), and behind that – itself invoked in Eliot's opening lines – Chaucer's 'Prologue' to *The Canterbury Tales*. Indeed, we may find here an explanation for Swift's seeming obsession with the month of April in *Last Orders* (and throughout his earlier fiction, too). The 'Prologue' famously begins with Chaucer's celebration of that month:

Whan that Aprill with his shoures soote [sweet showers]
The droghte [drought] of March hath perced [pierced] to the roote

. . . .

Thanne [then] longen folk to goon [go] on pilgrimages

. . . . . .

And specially from every shires end
Of Engelond to Caunterbury they wende,
The hooly blisful martir for to seke [seek]
That hem [them] hath holpen [helped] whan they were seeke [sick]

We may register immediately that, on 2 April 1990, the four
friends do indeed make a kind of 'pilgrimage' to Canterbury
where 'The hooly blissful martir' Thomas à Becket (remember the
pub they pass on the Old Kent Road) is buried, and Jack's ashes
are duly carried round the cathedral. It is also worth registering,
as outlined earlier, that all these men's lives have been and are
indeed 'sick'. But the first section of Eliot's poem – entitled, please
note, 'The Burial of the Dead' – opens with an implied rebuttal of
Chaucer's sense of the spiritually rejuvenating force of spring:

> April is the cruellest month, breeding
> Lilacs out of the dead land, mixing
> Memory and desire, stirring
> Dull roots with spring rain.
> Winter kept us warm, covering
> Earth in forgetful snow, feeding
> A little life with dried tubers.[4]

Here, April is the time when the return of feeling is painful, and
especially when reactivated 'memory' brings back the past from
a comforting 'forgetfulness'. As the four friends drive to Margate
(where they are indeed met by torrents of 'spring rain': 'the rain
starts to rain in earnest' (*LO* 290)), these 'little lives' are, of
course, *remembering* their past lives and the secrets (that is,
'forgettings') that have helped to make them 'sick', that are
painfully 'cruel', but that in some sense 'mix ... memory and
desire' (that embryonic desire for reconciliation that may help
them to become 'new people' – of which more below).

But before proceeding, let me further illustrate that *The Waste
Land* is a crucial intertext for *Last Orders* by indicating that it is
not just by references to April that Swift's novel invokes the
poem. It is surely no coincidence that Mandy, crossing London
Bridge early on a morning of 'wet murk', uses the word 'unreal'
about 'Cockney' voices, and then thinks: 'St Paul's, London
Bridge, the Tower, like things that weren't even real' (*LO* 161–2),
hence calling to mind Eliot's

> Unreal city,
> Under the brown fog of a winter dawn,
> A crowd flowed over London Bridge, so many,
> I had not thought death had undone so many

> (ll. 60–3)

87

– with its own allusion to Dante's *Inferno* when the poet observes the huge number of unhappy souls in hell who had known neither good nor evil while alive and had never cared for anyone but themselves. 'Unreality' is a recurrent aspect of Swift's contemporary 'hell', and his London here also seems to partake of it. Later, Amy, 'stuck in a mould' of bus journeys from London Bridge to visit June, thinks that, as long as 'a number 44' is running, 'the world won't fall apart, London Bridge won't fall down' (*LO* 230), again recalling one of the 'fragments' in the famous conclusion to Eliot's poem (ll. 426, 430). Furthermore, there are suggestive echoes in Swift's Coach and Horses, the pub that 'aint never gone nowhere', of the 'Cockney' pub scene in *The Waste Land* (ll. 139–72) – where the repeated and foreboding vocative 'HURRY UP PLEASE ITS TIME' has a similar duality of meaning to Swift's closing-time refrain of 'last orders'. This is reinforced when we remember that the women's conversation in the poem is partly about an abortion, and that Lenny has forced his daughter Sally to have the same – both texts using this to imply the sterility of the social worlds they are concerned with. In this context, then, even small details that might otherwise seem merely fortuitous begin to ring bells (does the fact that Ray's daughter has settled in Sydney recall Eliot's 'Mrs Porter and her daughter' (ll. 199–200), who derive from a ballad 'reported to me from Sydney, Australia'? (Eliot's 'Note' to l. 199)). More substantive, however, is the focus on Margate, where Eliot began *The Waste Land* in 1921 while convalescing from a breakdown and that appears in the poem as:

'On Margate Sands.
I can connect
Nothing with nothing.'

(ll. 300–2)

Late on in *Last Orders*, Amy thinks: 'by now [Jack]'ll be washed out to sea or mingling with Margate Sands' (*LO* 278), a cross reference surely reinforced by the fact that the fourth section of Eliot's poem is entitled 'Death by Water' and alludes to the anthropologist Jessie Weston's book *From Ritual to Romance* (1920). This cites pagan fertility rituals where a drowned god (in effigy) is later miraculously retrieved from the sea, hence proving the rebirth of the god and death-by-water as life bringing. Such retrievals would take place in the spring months (Easter is the Christian version of this) – thus giving 'April' further resonance.

But it is in the final scenes of *Last Orders* that the significance of invoking *The Waste Land* becomes most telling. The men are in Margate; they have seen the late-twentieth-century's vacuous citadel of pleasure, 'Dreamland'; the rain and sea spray are soaking them (*LO* 290–1; in Eliot's poem, water is simultaneously a symbol of fertility and redemption and an absence: 'the dry stone [gives] no sound of water' (l. 24)); they are on the pier ('One way there's Margate and Dreamland, the other there's the open sea' (*LO* 292)) with the casket of Jack's remains, from which they each take 'a handful/handfuls' of ashes (*LO* 193–4; earlier described as 'look[ing] like white dust' (*LO* 151)). 'Ashes to ashes, dust to dust', as the burial service has it: so what have we here then but 'a handful of dust' – one of the best-known images from Eliot's poem: 'I will show you fear in a handful of dust' (l. 30), and one usually taken to encapsulate the spiritual sterility of the 'wasteland' society of post-First World War Europe. In the novel, however, the handfuls of dust seem to represent some kind of expiation – a 'paying of dues' – associated as they are with purification by water, 'the heavens being about to open', as Ray puts it (*LO* 288), and 'the open sea' counterpointed with 'Dreamland'. As the last handfuls are scattered, and the novel ends, Ray muses, 'Jack Arthur Dodds, save our souls' (*LO* 294). Even so, neither *The Waste Land* nor *Last Orders* offers any positive final affirmation: the Fisher King in the former has 'the arid plane' behind him and asks whether he should 'at least set my lands in order' (ll. 424–5), while, although Jack's last 'order' has been fulfilled in the latter, any hints of possible redemption remain suspended – as in *Out of This World* – by the closure of the novel.

However, in one respect at least, Swift's April is at once just as 'cruel' as Eliot's and rather more hopeful. For the characters on 2 April 1990 are experiencing a stirring of 'memory and desire' that is leading them to *tell their stories* – even if as yet only mentally – to those they most want to be reconciled with and to propose to themselves actions that may break the 'mould' of their wasted lives and so become 'new people'. While Jack's mortal sickness and ultimate refusal to acknowledge June ('he's not going to say a word about her' (*LO* 267)) mean that any future for him and Amy remains stillborn (Ray thinks: 'it's a pretty poor starting-point [...] for becoming new people, a bungalow in Margate. It's not exactly the promised land' (*LO* 15)), at the end Jack is 'thinking of' Amy (*LO* 220). Vince admits about his daughter Kath: 'maybe I aint done right by her, maybe I aint' (*LO* 168); and when he lends his dying father £1,000, he thinks 'it's cleared my conscience', while Jack in turn 'comes to terms' with the 'son' who has rejected him by finally saying: 'You're a good boy, Vince' (*LO* 266). Lenny, the one who speaks of 'paying your dues' and 'making amends', is thinking – significantly in Canterbury Cathedral, where the 'hooly blisful martir' is buried – 'Maybe the first thing I ought to do after we've done our duty by Jack here is go and pay Sally a visit. It's me, girl. It's your old dad, *remember*?' (*LO* 209; emphasis added). For her part, after fifty fruitless years of hoping for some response from June, Amy is on her way to visit her for the last time: 'What I'm trying to say is Goodbye June. Goodbye Jack. They seem like one and the same thing.[...] I've got to think of my own future.[...] I've got to be my own woman now'; but pointedly, she has to '*tell*' June face-to-face about this decision and that Jack has died (*LO* 278). Ray, too, meditating about what to do with the 'secret' money he has won for Jack on the horse 'Miracle Worker' (*LO* 233 – does Swift's usual subtlety slip a little here?), thinks he could go to Australia to visit Susie, and 'I could say, I'm sorry. I'm sorry I stopped writing' (*LO* 281); he could take Amy with him and then 'own up' to Susie about their affair years before (*LO* 282); or he could simply inform Amy about the winnings, but 'then I can't see how I couldn't *tell* her. That it was sort of meant like a sign, like a permit, like a blessing on the two of us, to carry on where we left off' (*LO* 283; emphasis added). In the event, what Ray does do is '*tell*' Vince immediately before the scattering of Jack's ashes off Margate Pier: 'I've got your thousand. I'll give you back your thousand. I'll *explain*', and imply – in that familiar Swiftian phrase – that later he will tell Vince '*the full story*' (290; emphases added).

Of course, by now in our reading of Swift's fiction we know that there can never be 'the full story', for 'secrets' – or 'holes' – always remain: Vic never told Jack about Amy and Ray's affair – nor did Amy herself – and Ray will never know for certain whether Jack or Vince knew about it either. Perhaps more to the point, for the reader of the novel, is the fact that we are 'told' nothing of what happens after 2 April 1990, nothing of whether expiation achieves anything, nothing of whether redemption results, nothing of whether the characters pursue 'new lives', become 'new people'. Despite Ray's late conviction about Jack – 'But then *he* knew all along' – and his sense that Jack on his deathbed is bequeathing Amy to him – 'As if he was saying, These are my shoes, Raysy, go on, step in 'em, wear 'em.[...] You and Ame' (*LO* 283) – we never know what happens to Ray's winnings, whether Jack's death means that Ray and Amy 'get a second chance [...] start up again just when you think it's finished' (*LO* 252), or whether Ray goes to Australia with Amy, by himself, or not at all. Instead, and characteristically, we are left with Ray's equivocal valediction – immediately prior to Jack's 'wastage' section – in which he can salvage only a *memory* of 'desire': of him and Amy at a racetrack in the camper van in 1967:

> The sea's the colour of desertion. It's the colour of wet ash. The rain's coming. Oh Ray, you're a lovely man. To have lived and heard a woman say that to you, even if it aint true. You're a lovely man. The rain on the roof, the noise of the crowd like waves. With tears in her eyes and a flame in her throat: Oh Ray, you're a lovely man, you're a lucky man, you're a little ray of sunshine, you're a little ray of hope. (*LO* 284)

Everything is equivocal here: from the colour of the sea, through the water imagery of rain, tears and waves, to the potential for happiness ('lovely man', 'lucky man', 'ray of sunshine', 'ray of hope') – 'even if it aint true'. All the novel seems to confirm once more is that in the Dreamland–Wasteland of the late twentieth century only 'telling' offers the chance of redemption: by bringing the 'secrets' of wasted lives into 'the light of day'.

6

The Light of Day

Graham Swift's long-awaited most recent novel (published in February 2003 – seven years after *Last Orders*) seems to be, almost unnervingly, pure Swift: as though he has been rendering his work down to a reduced and clarified essence. When it first appeared, one reviewer noted that the geographical area the novel covers had shrunk to a specific part of south London (Wimbledon/Putney Vale) and Chislehurst in Kent,[1] but it is also much reduced in chronological scope, with the end of the Second World War just creeping in but most of the principal events taking place in the late 1980s and 1990s and with 'the present' once more comprising a single day, 20 November 1997. Even so, the relationship between the events, and the 'explanation' for why they occur, is subject to what we might now call Swift's 'slow-release' mode of narration, with small fragments of 'what really happened' being offered the reader in an unhurried, non-linear and apparently piecemeal fashion. Furthermore, Swift has returned to a single male narrator; introduces no other characters than ones who are largely absent for some reason (dead, in prison, have walked out); and has further honed his style in order, as he put it in an interview, to 'make ordinary simple words do extraordinary things'[2] – of which the following is a brief example: 'Late October. The clocks about to go back. Now more things could happen in the dark' (*LD* 29). But what is even more striking is that some of these 'ordinary simple words' are again the ones that have tolled so regularly throughout his previous fiction: 'tell/not tell', 'know/not know', 'real/unreal', 'secrets', 'love', 'stories', 'whole stories', 'writing'. And either because we are over-attuned to Swift's writing by now or because of the pared-down style, they seem to be even more inescapably present than hitherto. So is Swift just working the same old vein, albeit with even greater writerly finesse (a little bit of ivory two inches wide?), or is he developing his themes, even taking a different focus?

20 November 1997 – 'today's a special day' (*LD* 3) – is the second anniversary of the stabbing to death of her husband, Bob, a successful gynaecologist, by Sarah Nash, a college lecturer, who for the past two years has been serving a life sentence in a women's prison as a result. George Webb, the narrator, is a disgraced policeman, now a private detective, who was recruited by Sarah in October 1995 to keep her husband and his young Croatian lover, Kristina Lazic, under surveillance in order to make sure that Kristina did indeed catch a plane back to Croatia alone on 20 November 1995. George, already half in love with Sarah before the murder, now centres his life around her, visits her in prison every Thursday (like Amy in *Last Orders*, he has become 'this – visitor' (*LD* 123) to yet another incarcerated woman), and is spending 'today' placing flowers on Bob's grave at Putney Vale crematorium on Sarah's behalf, visiting Sarah herself, and driving by the desirable suburban house where the murder took place two years before. And that is about it – except, of course, that into the bare threads of this story are woven the fabric of past lives that will 'explain' why Sarah did it, 'what really happened', and why, as George's assistant, Rita, says to him in the first line of the novel, 'Something's come over you' (*LD* 3): will give us, in other words, 'the full story, the whole story' (*LD* 21). It may be helpful once again, therefore, to sketch in and point up the history of these lives, which is scattered around the text.

Leaving aside for now the presence in the novel of Emperor Napoleon III and his wife, Empress Eugenie, who lived in exile in Chislehurst, Kent, after their forced departure from France in 1870, the first significant date is 1946, just after the Second World War had ended, when George's dad, Frank Webb, still in the army and posted to Germany, is taught how to use a camera in order to 'take photos of displaced persons, to go in the records [...] Displaced persons, no shortage of them. "That was his job [...] Someone had to do it"' (*LD* 229). Thus the fallout from the war is once again flagged, if only vestigially ('displaced persons' will, however, play a significant part in the present of the novel, too), and photography – already problematized in *Out of This*

World – is also a prominent motif here. On leaving the army in 1946, Frank becomes a beach photographer in Broadstairs ('How to snap and make them smile. A camera and a bit of army know-how' (*LD* 229)), where he meets George's mum, Jane: 'He knew how to make *me* smile. My God, he could make me smile' (*LD* 83) – and 'smiles' combined with photographs will become yet another motif of specious 'realism', another simulacrum of 'the real thing'. They marry 'late in 1946', and George is born the following year (*LD* 80). Frank progresses to high-street photography in Lewisham, and in 1952 the family move to Chislehurst, where Frank becomes 'A pillar of the community. More than that: its record keeper, its curator.[...] His name on all those memory lanes' – 'Smile!' (*LD* 80). I will return later to what kind of 'pillar' of what kind of 'community' Frank is, and to the nature of those photographic 'records' of the 'memory lanes' of Chislehurst's 'better class of customer' (*LD* 80).

In 1965, George joins the police force (*LD* 120), serving in it for twenty-four years (*LD* 97) until his disgrace and expulsion in 1989 (see below), and in 1968 (*LD* 90), as a plain-clothes detective, he meets Rachel, a trainee teacher and his wife-to-be – in April, of course: 'Outside the rain was pelting. April – Easter coming up[...] Then the rain was suddenly stopping [...] A gleam in the sky' (*LD* 88; powerful echoes here of that equivocally redemptive moment at the end of *Last Orders*). They fall instantly in love; marry 'early in '69' (*LD* 90); and have a daughter, Helen, who is in her twenties in the novel's 'present'. Frank Webb dies in 1986 – once more in April (*LD* 120: surely this is 'the cruellest month'), followed by George's mother in 1989 – his *annus horribilis* – although some months before he 'was kicked out of the Force': 'So *they* never knew, neither of them, about *my* scandal and disgrace' (*LD* 123). As we shall see, there is a great deal of 'not knowing' in George's 'full story'. In September 1989 (*LD* 110), during the interrogation of two suspects accused of stabbing an Asian shopkeeper in the chest (unlike Sarah's stabbing of Bob, this one is not fatal), George 'sees red' (*LD* 119) and assaults one of the prisoners in front of his solicitor. As a result, neither suspect can be charged, and George 'got the axe' (*LD* 134): 'The word that got used was "corrupt".[...] As if they've rooted out some foul stuff inside you and it's you, it's yours now, you're stuck with it for good.[...] the air was busy in those days with the word "corrupt"' (LD 134). Indeed, 'corruption', in one shape or form, taints much of the world of *The Light of Day* – the novel's characteristically apt title suggesting that George's 'his-story' will bring it precisely out from 'the dark' and into – the light of day. His wife ('she'd grown sick of my smell.[...] The taint *was* me' (LD 135)) immediately and abruptly leaves him: 'As if [...] it had all been [...] like some long, non-stop test which I'd finally failed. Teachers! Don't you just love them?' (LD 71; the irony here is that George will later 'love' another 'teacher' – who turns out to be a murderess). Thereafter, he has no contact with Rachel – she absents herself completely from his life, the only positive result being a reconciliation between George and his estranged daughter, whom on occasion his narrative seems to be addressing (e.g. LD 86), and of whom he claims: 'I've told Helen most things now, of course, most of the story' (LD 47). Whether or not he has is, 'of course', impossible for us to know – especially as most of George's narrative is clearly *not* addressed to Helen, as his use of the third person, and not the second, indicates (e.g. LD 193). When young, Helen had always 'hated' George (LD 41, 46), and in another of Swift's damaged father–daughter relationships (cf. *Last Orders*), George thinks of them, pointedly, as 'the two of us *at war*' (LD 215; emphasis added). But, with Rachel's departure, Helen gets to know 'this dad of hers that she'd never known' (LD 190), just as he begins to know 'this [...] daughter [...] who you hardly know' (LD 95). In 'the present', however, with 'this woman in my life.[...] this prisoner. This killer', George confesses (to whom?): 'Helen, I think, doesn't understand me any more, not these days' (LD 215). And, indeed, one of the central questions the novel poses for us is how do *we* 'understand' George's obsessive love for the unattainable Sarah (he has no idea when she will be released from prison (LD 18)).

In 1995, Bob and Sarah Nash have been married for twenty-four years (LD 183), and 'He wasn't a "womanizer".[...] There wasn't a history. Just the history of them being a happy couple with good careers' (LD 32). But, late in 1993, Sarah begins to take under her wing Kristina Lazic, a Croatian student whose visa would soon expire and who would then have to register as an asylum-seeker or be forced to return to her war-ravaged country. The Nashs decide to take her in, and she moves into their 'smart house in Wimbledon' (*LD* 34) 'in September, three years ago' (*LD* 36; i.e. 1994). Later, Sarah intuits that her husband and Kristina are having a passionate sexual affair; Bob 'confesses' (*LD* 57); and, as a 'concession' by Sarah (*LD* 67), he is allowed to rent a flat in Fulham for Kristina, where he sleeps with her for the last few weeks before her finally agreed departure for Croatia in the autumn of 1995. In late October, Sarah visits George to ask if he will shadow the couple to Heathrow, where Bob is going to see Kristina off: 'To see if she really goes.[...] Will you follow them and watch them and tell me what happens?' (*LD* 15). On 20 November 1995, then, while Kristina does indeed catch her plane alone and Bob does head back to Sarah in Wimbledon, George, as we shall see, does not 'tell' Sarah 'what [really] happens' – especially in relation to Bob. When he telephones to say, 'She's gone by herself.[...] Everything's all right.[...] He's on his way home to you', he adds: 'I lied' (*LD* 158–9). For Bob, although physically 'on his way home', is 'like a man who'd forgotten who he was' (*LD* 159), is 'already, a ghost' (*LD* 181). When he arrives home to Sarah, 'it's as though there's nothing left of him inside, he's drained away. She sees it' (*LD* 227), and it is then that she stabs him through the heart with a kitchen knife, immediately afterwards telephoning the police to say ' "I did it". End of case, end of story' (*LD* 225).

But not, of course, 'end of story' at all. Back in October 1995, having asked George 'So you want to know the story?' while briefing him on what she wants him to do in respect of Bob's affair, Sarah uses a resonant metaphor in the Swift lexicon: 'I didn't want to go to war, George. I didn't want to make a war of it.[...] What I'd say is – if you're going to be unhappy, better an unhappy peace than an unhappy war.[...] Not war but – intelligence' (*LD* 69). For, while the Second World War is no longer any more than a vestigial presence in *The Light of Day*, one of the typically understated contexts the novel sets up around the comfort and prosperity of life in Wimbledon or Chislehurst is that invoked by the war refugee, Kristina Lazic. The civil war in the former Yugoslavia, especially that between Serbs and Croats, was partly the result of bitter hostility between them in the Second World War and was ruthlessly pursued by both sides during the 1990s. It is no surprise, then, that Kristina – herself a 'displaced person' (we might recall Frank Webb's job at the end of the Second World War) – is yet another of Swift's 'children of war', albeit this time of a more contemporary one: 'the world she'd left behind her had been smashed apart.[...] First her brother, then both her parents had been killed' (*LD* 33). She is 'a damaged soul, a convalescent, a stunted flower' (*LD* 35), but one who is transplanted to the rich earth of – well, Wimbledon, and there 'she'd bloomed' (*LD* 35). But what as? A poisonous plant, 'tainted' by the 'corruption' of war? – one who sows her own seeds of destruction in 'this home-and-garden land, this never-never land where nothing much is ever meant to happen. These Wimbledons and Chislehursts' (*LD* 19), 'This safe-as-houses land where nothing is meant to disturb the peace' (*LD* 21)? George muses:

> all the time – she must have thought it: I might have been there and not here. I might be dead too, worse than dead. I might have had to watch while they shot the others first, raped the others first, then shot them. She'd always know it. But here she was in a warm bed in Wimbledon. Lawns and trees. Where were the rules now? (*LD* 58)

And, as Kristina flies home, he tries to imagine what she does or does not know: 'And she didn't know – how could she?[...] the destruction she'd left behind. But then – she'd always been leaving destruction behind. The story of her life. Five years in England while everything she'd known was torn apart. Going back now to see what was left' (*LD* 106). 'The story of her life': and of others, too; for the contaminations of war do not merely rest with those directly affected – nor the culpability for them. 'These Wimbledons and Chislehursts' are implicated, too.

What, then, are the attitudes of the inhabitants of Wimbledon to Kristina and war in the former Yugoslavia? George surmises the kinds of reactions Sarah's decision to take her in might meet:

> Charity: okay if you've got the money, if you've got the room. Okay for some. A luxury item. And was it such a fine piece of charity anyway, if what you got out of it was an unpaid help around the home and the bonus of feeling good? Look, we have everything – including our very own orphaned Croatian maid. Look at the good life we lead. (*LD* 34)

Even more telling is Sarah's entirely selfish response to Kristina's 'going back [...] to where they've ditched all the rules' (*LD* 142):

> 'I blessed the day when the Croats started fighting back, pushing back the Serbs, and the whole thing looked like it could soon be over. I thought this could be my – our solution. I wanted to cheer them on. Never mind they were killing each other, never mind they were doing as bad things to the Serbs as the Serbs had done to them. I was on their side! Our solution. [...] Crazy, isn't it? Wanting a war to be won just so it might save your day.[...] Appalling, isn't it? And it all happened. I mean, it happened *my* way.[...] In her own country. Back where she belongs. Terrible, isn't it?' (*LD* 74)

George makes no comment, but the appropriate response to Sarah's questions surely is: yes, absolutely 'appalling', absolutely 'terrible' – how can safe citizens of Wimbledon hold such callously self-serving and inhumane views: 'Back where she belongs', indeed. And much later, George thinks that Bob 'wanted that war – out there – to go on forever. Or wanted the Croats to get beaten, smashed – so she might ditch the idea of one day returning. Not caring about killing and maiming. And him in a caring profession.[...] Better an unhappy war ...' (*LD* 198). Not for nothing is *The Light of Day*'s epigraph '*All's fair in love and war*' – although its full and bitter irony is released only as the reader reaches passages where 'a caring professional's' self-interest makes him hope the Croats 'get [...] smashed' and that of his cultivated wife the reverse.

But it is not just the individual participants who are guilty of myopic disregard for 'an unhappy war' in another country. As George drives past the Nashs' old house in Wimbledon, he wonders if the residents remember the murder two years previously: or is it 'forgotten? Deliberately wiped from the record? A missing file. No, not here. You must be thinking of somewhere else. Streets in Dubrovnik. In Croatian villages' (*LD* 203). 'Wimbledon', 'this safe-as-houses land where nothing is meant to disturb the peace', is responsible for deliberate amnesia – 'forgetting' – so that its 'peace' may be preserved, although, as we shall see, such a peace is itself specious. And 'forgetting', we may recall from previous novels, is what people did after the First and Second World Wars – with dire consequences. One telling example of this out-of-sight-out-of-mind mentality is exemplified in George's reflections on Kristina 'leaving destruction behind' quoted earlier, followed by the question: 'Hard-eyed and hardened?[...] You'd look and think: no child. A woman of the world.[...] Oh she knew how to turn everything to havoc.[...] Atrocities on both sides. Fair's fair' – in love and war, we may add (*LD* 106–7). And he concludes: 'What became of her?[...] I could follow her too, track her down.[...] Find out the truth: did she ever *know*? But ... that's not my case' (*LD* 108–9). George's wilful ignorance and careless indifference about Kristina and her fate, together with his partiality ('that's not my case' – his is Sarah's), mean that he will not 'find out the truth': that 'the whole picture, the whole story' (*LD* 224) he believes he is conveying (without Sarah, he thinks, 'I might [...] never have learnt the full story' (*LD* 22)) will once again contain some resounding 'holes'. But then, as we shall see later, in this novel George is a truly 'unreliable' narrator. One final comment of his about Kristina will lead us to what I see as the novel's prime focus. George says, again uncharitably: 'she went back with her loot, her credentials, a veteran of the English suburbs' (*LD* 107). That final phrase is a wonderful inversion of what we might expect: 'a veteran' suggests someone who has extensive experience of war – how then 'a veteran of the English suburbs'? The implication must be that the 'peace' of 'these Wimbledons and Chislehursts' is a dangerous fiction, a fantasy ('a never-never land'), which belies the 'secrets' of 'corruption' and betrayal lurking just below the surface, 'in the dark', out of 'the clear light of day' (*LD* 244). If anything has 'hardened' Kristina, it was experiencing the spoilt, careless and destructive 'good life' of 'the English suburbs' juxtaposed with 'the real thing' in Croatia, a 'good life' indifferent to the plight of her own country except in so far as it impacts on their affairs of love and war – or rather, love *as* war.

When asked what his plays were about, Harold Pinter once replied: 'The weasel under the cocktail cabinet',[3] a brilliant metaphor for the lurking menace of feral drives and impulses just below the veneer of civilization. In his turn, Graham Swift, in a second interview when *The Light of Day* was published, characteristically remarked: 'There's more there than meets the eye'.[4] It seems to me that the major thrust of the novel – albeit never foregrounded – is to take the lid off 'the English suburbs', to pull their cosseted selfishness and corruption into 'the light of day'. In a sense, of course, the murky lives of lower-middle-class England have always been Swift's subject, but never so centrally and bitterly as in the present novel. That this is its focus is perhaps obscured initially by the fact that it is narrated by George, who, I suggest, is himself 'unreliable' precisely because he is so besotted by Sarah, the quintessential suburban woman, and because the 'picture' of suburbia he gives us is not in itself ironic: it is, rather, Swift's irony that plays over both him and it. Once perceived, however, suburbia and its secrets are everywhere apparent as the novel's prey.

Thinking about Chislehurst before the golf course was built, George muses: 'And Chislehurst then, like Wimbledon, would have been more or less a village in the country, not yet conquered by the suburbs. London on the march. The empire of suburbs' (*LD* 235) – phrases surely reminiscent of E. M. Forster's similar perception in his 'Condition of England' novel, *Howards End* (1910), of the 'red rust' of suburbia 'ceeping' over the countryside from London[5]). And this 'empire of the suburbs' – 'this home-and-garden land, this never-never land', 'this safe-as-houses land', this land of 'peace' – is also very exclusive: 'A cul-de-sac with verges and chain-links and houses screened by autumn trees. It could almost be a private road. Private, keep out: not for you' (*LD* 26). But its very privacy hides its secrets: 'All the windows, saying nothing, lights on, lights off. All the houses that stare at each other across streets. Read my face, guess what I've got inside' (*LD* 124). Later, George uses a significant trope to suggest how 'what they've got inside' might be accessed:

> Lift off the roofs of houses, lift up their lids, and what would you see? What would the aggregate be? More misery and hatred than you could begin to imagine? Or more secret happiness, more goodness and mercy than you ever could have guessed? But no one can do that, can they? So how do we know? Lift off the roofs of houses, peer inside. Except the police. Police – open up. (*LD* 209)

And, we might hazard – except for novelists. In Swiftland, 'the aggregate' is surely 'more misery and hatred' than 'secret happiness', where, as George puts it, 'I've seen quite a few couples who've come to grief, who've *gone to war*, for no other other reason [...] than that over the years of being safe and steady and settled, something's got lost, something's gone missing, they've got bored' (*LD* 217; emphasis added). Sarah 'didn't want to go to war' over Bob's affair with Kristina, we may remember; but 'in a nice clean home – not just a nice clean home but a pricey pad in the leafiest, choicest part of Wimbledon ...' (*LD* 160), Bob gets killed and Kristina becomes 'a veteran of the English suburbs'. The 'good life' may not be all it seems.

Late on in the novel (Swift seldom forces these motifs upon us), George remembers 'The Chislehurst Caves':

> First there'd been a village among the fields, then a suburb, with a high street and golf course, but before all that there'd been the caves: a whole network of them [...] No one knew how they'd first got there. An unsolved mystery, disappearing into the dark [...] The echoes, the maze of tunnels, the stories of ghosts. The feeling that you might never get back into the light. The caves ran everywhere. They must have run under our house. Under the golf course. (*LD* 237–8)

The imagery here ('unsolved mystery', 'into the dark', 'maze', 'ghosts', 'never get back into the light') suggests that, beneath the high street, the golf course and the Webb family's home, suburban Chislehurst is riddled with a whole 'dark network' of secrets. But the significance of the caves increases when we learn that 'the one undisputed fact' about them is that they were used as 'a natural shelter [...] In the air raids in the war': 'Thousands of people, apparently [...] It's hard to imagine. Chislehurst had gone underground' *LD* (238): Chislehurst touched by the Second World War; Chislehurst 'gone underground' (we might remember that trope in *Shuttlecock*, too). And who is the main figuration of suburban betrayal and deception here but that 'pillar of the community [...] its record keeper, its curator', Frank Webb (scarcely 'frank' as it turns out). For 'he was in the smile trade, and they weren't *real*, half those smiles, just the trick of the moment. His job, his challenge: to get the smile, no matter the mood, the resistance, the reluctance. And there it would be, fixed in black and white, a glossy finish, as if it were true and for always: a smile' (228; emphasis added). 'The smile trade': one thinks here of Beech senior in *Out of This World* with his joke about being in the 'arms trade' because of his collection of artificial limbs, and of Harry's sense of the falsification of 'the real thing' by a photographic simulacrum. But in 'the empire of suburbia', such an image also has 'a glossy

101

finish, as if it were true'. Pointedly, we learn elsewhere that even a couple who 'had had a bust-up that very day' could be made to smile by Frank, and that in 'missing person' enquiries his portrait photographs might be used – but 'sometimes there seems to be only the one. The one that shows the two of them together, beaming and never to be parted' (LD 80–1). The camera, of course, never lies (think of *Out of This World* once more), so those 'records' of 'memory lanes' in suburban Chislehurst must indeed be *telling stories*.

Chislehurst's golf course plays a significant role in *The Light of Day*. It is while caddying for Frank as a boy that George learns his father is having an affair with another woman, a discovery that leads to a lifetime of 'pretending' (LD 82): 'I'd have to pretend – so Mum would never know.[...] Pretend, keep silence' (LD 99). As a result, George also begins a life of sleuthing, keeping under surveillance those 'partners in secrecy', Frank and his lover Carol, as they meet up in an empty house (she works for an estate agent): 'And this was their only shelter, here in Collingwood Road?', or did they have, he wonders, 'a whole string of shelters, in Chislehurst, in Petts Wood, in Bromley, all round the not-to-be-trusted suburbs?' (LD 102; notice how 'shelters' picks up the description of an 'underground' Chislehurst in the caves). George, in the 'not-to-be-trusted suburbs', no longer has 'a *real* home any more, *just a pretend one*' (LD 102; emphases added), but he never 'tells' his mother he knew about the affair ('she never knew I knew. I'm proud of that' (LD 123)): even after Frank, on his deathbed, mutters Carol's name several times in their hearing, 'I never said a thing' (LD 121). What he does do is carry out his mother's wish for a public bench to be placed on Chislehurst Common with the names 'Frank and Jane' on it – a public fiction of the fidelity of their relationship, rather like one of Frank's 'glossy' photographs showing a ('warring') couple 'never to be parted'. In this 'whole story' of equivocal 'telling' and 'knowing', it is significant also that George never tells Sarah about Frank's affair: 'I've never told Sarah – I don't know why, since it's what really makes *the story* [...] I just told Sarah about the bench' (LD 228–9; emphasis added). So 'the story' Sarah gets from George is the fiction of his parents' 'never-to-be-partedness': these 'not-to-be-trusted suburbs', indeed.

A close reading of *The Light of Day* – starting with its opening short paragraphs and evidenced by the quotations above – will reveal an extraordinary repetition of the words 'know' and 'tell', with barely a page passing where one or other or both are not used. But most often they occur in a negative sense: for example as (echoing earlier novels), 'maybe it's best not to know' (*LD* 78), 'Some things it's best not to know' (*LD* 107), 'Don't mention it, not a word' (*LD* 207), 'I've never told [...] I don't tell her [...]' (*LD* 154–5). For the 'not-to-be-trusted suburbs', as the case of Frank Webb shows, are replete with secrecy and deception: a world where George's clients 'enter a little web of deceit' *(LD* 40) and are not required to give 'the full story, the whole story.[...] they don't have to tell you that' (*LD* 21). But 'the whole story' most full of 'holes' here is George's own – certainly as far as Sarah is concerned. In addition to not telling her about his father's infidelity, he won't tell her that he has not burnt all her personal possessions as she asked: 'I'm their secret curator now' (*LD* 18); nor that he has slept with his assistant: 'I haven't told Sarah everything about Rita [...] But she knows, I know she knows [...] It's a game we play.[...] A game of jealousy'; nor that Rita is about to quit working for him: 'But I know this isn't the time to tell her'; and he concludes: 'I haven't told Sarah everything. Does anyone tell anyone everything? There are things I can't and won't tell Sarah yet. Perhaps I never will' (*LD* 174–6). One of the main 'things' George 'never told Sarah' (*LD* 178 – nor the police inspector in charge of her murder case: 'But I wasn't going to tell him. Some things are best left unsaid' (*LD* 196)) is that he followed her husband on his way back from seeing Kristina off at Heathrow, thus witnessing how Bob came within an inch of killing himself in a traffic accident, and how he then revisited the love nest in Fulham for fifteen minutes where George was again concerned he would commit suicide (*LD* 179–80, 185): 'Can I ever tell her? That he went to the flat first? Not straight home.[...] Some things are best never known.[...] How can I tell her?' (*LD* 201). Hence, despite Sarah's tuition in 'words' and 'writing' (*LD* 131, 228), George's 'twice-monthly reports from the world' to Sarah in prison (*LD* 138 – 'Write it down for me [...] what it's like out there. Bring the world in here' (*LD* 188)) are in fact no more than 'stories' – and certainly not 'full' or 'whole' ones at that. Pointedly, another phrase that riffs through

George's narrative is that 'You have to put yourself into the picture [...] You have to picture the scene' (*LD* 59–60 – of Bob and Kristina having sex on Wimbledon Common), or alternatively, 'You have to put youself in the scene' (*LD* 87, 184). In other words, George, like Bill Unwin in *Ever After*, has to imagine or 'make up' the situations he can have no other way of knowing about. And 'telling stories', as we are now fully aware in Swift's fiction, are deeply ambiguous ways of knowing.

The central point here is that in this novel George seems to be a truly unreliable narrator: in the sense that he unwittingly reveals more than he is aware of – most particularly because what he regards as his grasp of 'the whole picture, the whole story' (*LD* 224) is deeply *partial* in both senses of the word (at once incomplete and subjectively angled). And the principal cause of this partiality is his blind infatuation with Sarah. Even though she is beyond reach (she is, after all, in prison), and even though he is unsure whether she still loves Bob or not ('It's only natural: to kill the man you love – love? loved?' (*LD* 146)), George's whole life now centres around her. Pointedly, he describes the moment he realizes he is in love with her (immediatcly after she has stabbed Bob): 'And if I hadn't known it before (but I did), I knew it now. If I hadn't felt it before, I felt it now. A stab to the heart' (*LD* 219). In the context, that final phrase is chilling. Significantly, his hitherto loyal and supportive daughter Helen 'doesn't understand me any more, not these days.[...] This woman in my life [...] this prisoner. This killer' (*LD* 215). But it is George's assistant, Rita, who most uncompromisingly tries to break his infatuation: 'Rita said it couldn't go on – this nonsense. She was *telling* me for my own good.[...] "Grow up, George. Get bloody *real*." Someone had to *tell* me. It couldn't go on' (*LD* 231; emphases added). And, in my view, it is Rita rather than Sarah who is the 'heroine' of *The Light of Day*. On the first occasion she meets George, she gets him to accompany her to the house where her estranged husband is living: 'I'll never know what she did or said in there, but she walked out in a way that was magnificent' (*LD* 191); she then spontaneously and unselfconsciously seduces George (*LD* 192). He thinks of her as 'a *real* find' and her talent for 'undercover work' not 'just a fancy, it was *real*' (*LD* 194; emphases added). But Rita, this direct, efficient, capable and clear-sighted woman who is in touch with

'the real', is about to leave him – to Sarah. In this context, then, it
crucial to hear what Rita thinks of Sarah: 'she didn't have to do
it, did she?' (LD 220); 'A piece of work, if you ask me, that Mrs
Nash. A nasty piece of work' (LD 222). Thinking earlier about
how people would view 'The Nash Case' after the murder,
George surmises: '[Bob] didn't look so pretty. But who was the
real monster now?' (LD 166). In spite of George's biased
narrative (Sarah, after all, is its guiding light: 'The truth is she's
taught me [...] to say all this, to put things down in words' (LD
8)), the answer is clear: 'the *real* monster' is that 'nasty piece of
work', Sarah Nash, that 'not-to-be-trusted' goddess of 'the
empire of the suburb': as the novel repeats, 'you never know
what you have inside ...' (LD 205), 'These unsuspected people
inside us' (LD 194). Wimbledon and Croatia are, after all, not so
far apart.

One thing Rita is no good at is cooking: 'she's a hopeless
cook' (LD 6, 194), the inverse significance of which lies in the
novel's equation of cooking with the kind of selfish and
possessive 'love' suburbia breeds. For despite Sarah's pious
protestation – and George's repetition of it thereafter – 'To love
is to be ready to lose – isn't it? It's not to have, it's not to keep.
It's to put someone else's happiness before yours. Isn't that how
it should be?' (LD 69) – that isn't quite how it turns out to be
here: if Sarah has lost Bob, then no one else is having him. It is
not without point, then, that Sarah and Bob 'fell in love, really in
love [...] over *coq au vin*' (LD 162), which is also the meal Sarah is
cooking for Bob's home-coming on the fatal evening of 20
November 1995 (George's narrative hovers lovingly over its
preparation in the latter part of the novel) – a dish, therefore,
that can presage two versions of 'a stab to the heart'. George,
intensely proud of his own cooking prowess, calls it his 'little
private passion', and when he accosts Sarah in the classy
supermarket after their first meeting, he reflects: 'Cooking. It
was something for her too, a bit of a thing, a passion' (LD 22).
But just prior to this, he makes a parenthetical aside that
resonates unmistakably in the Swift universe: '(And it's a well-
known substitute)' (LD 22). Haute cuisine, in other words, has
become a 'substitoot' in modern suburbia for 'love' – hence the
significance of Rita's inability to cook, a woman whose 'passion',
given half the chance, would be for 'the real thing'. But, in the

event, George is beguiled by the siren of suburbia and the ersatz delights on the menu of contemporary civilization. At one point, he muses: 'Chicken Marsala, followed by lemon tart. A bottle of wine. A man and a woman at a candlelit table. Interior design. Don't knock it – what's civilization for?' (*LD* 98). Our sense here is that the irony is Swift's rather than the 'unreliable' George's, and that final question, slightly modified, is reiterated throughout the novel: 'Public benches, golf courses. What's civilization for?' (*LD* 123). Earlier, George quotes his father's belief that 'where there were golf courses there was civilization and where there was civilization there were golf courses', adding: 'What would my mum have thought? Where there were department stores? Park benches? And Helen? Where there was Art? Interior design?' (*LD* 235–6). Of the 'leafy, looked-after, quiet zone' where the Nashs' house is, George says: 'And don't knock it anyway.[...] These Wimbledons and Chislehursts. What else is civilization for?' (*LD* 19 – although the phrase 'quiet zone' inversely suggests that 'war' is not far off); of 'the good life, the sweet life, windows lit at night. Peace? Excitement? What's civilization for?' (*LD* 217). While George, in thrall to Sarah, appreciates 'the good life, the sweet life' of suburbia, we are surely led to ask: is this *all* 'civilization' means? Safety and freedom to pursue one's selfish interests while Croatia burns? Golf courses patronized by men in the meretricious 'smile trade'? The 'empire of suburbia' where love becomes war and cooking becomes a 'substitoot' for love, where a 'Tanning Centre' – 'Tans in winter, sunshine in the dark' – inverts reality (*LD* 239), and where private eyes make their living from pampered people who 'can still (you'd be surprised) do the strangest things' (*LD* 19)? An introverted consumerist 'Dreamland' no longer redeemed by even the 'stories' it generates? 'Now everything we do will be in the dark', George remarks as the autumn nights draw in (*LD* 188); what Swift leaves unclear is wherein lies the possibility for a return of 'the light of day'.

What then, finally, of the shadowy presence in the novel of Emperor Napoleon III of France and his wife, Empress Eugenie, in whom both George and Sarah are interested? They belong to 'a different world, a different age' (*LD* 184), an age when 'Chislehurst then, like Wimbledon, would have been more or less a village in the country, not yet *conquered* by the suburbs' (*LD* 235; emphasis added), an age before 'the grounds of their home, their place of exile, [were] turned into a golf course' (*LD* 237). Swift makes no overt comparisons between then and now, nor between Eugenie and Sarah (although Napoleon, too, 'used to play around [...] Other women' (*LD* 236)), but the presence of the historical emperor and empress nevertheless suggests a world other than that of 'the empire of the suburbs'. Furthermore, rather in the way Swift used the Matthew Pearce story in *Ever After*, there is a sense that Eugenie represents the kind of integrity that contemporary suburbia lacks: 'Strong-minded, ambitious, beautiful. But devoted.[...] she staked her life on him' (*LD* 236), and for whom, during the fifty years she survived her husband, 'there was no one else. She never remarried. No one to take the Emperor's place' (*LD* 237). Those fifty years are 'the part that draws Sarah, I know', muses George (*LD* 237); and thus a large question mark hangs over whether Sarah will in time become, like Eugenie, 'a plucky, feisty, not-so-old bird, ready to have a go' (*LD* 237) who yet remains 'devoted' and faithful to *her* dead emperor, or whether she will find a 'substitoot' in George and pastiche cooking – Chicken Marsala, *coq au vin* ('forget a *real* cock, in Wimbledon' (*LD* 161; emphasis added)) – in the 'safe-as-houses land' of suburbia and its phoney peace.

Conclusion

Reading contemporary writing is a rather different exercise from reading texts that come from earlier literary periods, in that it means attaining a different kind of historical sense: a sense not of reconstructing the past in which an older text was written, but of grasping the contemporary text's present historical moment as it is being lived and experienced. In other words, to read Graham Swift's fiction requires us to situate it in its own cultural ambience and to try and decipher what it tells us about – and what positions it takes up towards – the world that determines it and that it addresses. This implies a more immediately engaged mode of reading: what we may call a 'politics of reading'. As we have seen, the world that Swift's novels invoke is that of 'the present' as a postmodern wasteland: indelibly marked by destructive twentieth-century wars; consumerist, careless and selfish; dominated by factitious images on film and TV; emotionally null – with 'love' a prime casualty; the possibility of reaching any certain 'truth' a chimera; overshadowed by the necessarily vicarious 'experiencing' of nuclear holocaust; and with 'the End of History' nigh. Our decision (implying its 'politics') about how to respond to this world view is central to a reading of Swift's fiction.

For we are left to judge whether the world the texts allude to is one we can square with the world we experience in our daily lives – whether we think: 'no, this is merely the jaundiced view of an over-fastidious novelist alienated from the dynamics of contemporary culture'; or alternatively: 'yes, that is how it seems; I can recognize and identify with that'. But what is equally a part of our 'politics of reading' is how we react to the *challenges* the novels offer to their prevailing contextual world, for Swift does not merely identify a contemporary wasteland but seems to suggest an antidote to it. And the central possibility for redemption (apart from 'telling stories'), put very simply, is 'love' – if only as a minimal and vulnerable eventuality. However, it is worth bearing in mind that, with a sophisticated, self-conscious novelist like Swift, all his representations of the contextualizing world are those of his first-person narrators, and can therefore never be taken unproblematically to be the unmediated views of the author. Swift, in other words, can always escape the accusation that *he* may feel like this by reminding us that it is Tom Crick, Harry Beech, Bill Unwin, Ray Johnson or George Webb who is 'speaking'. What I propose to do here in conclusion, then – while acknowledging my profound admiration for Swift's fiction – is raise two related problems that seem to traverse it. These are: (1) the status of the novels' (principally male) first-person narrators; and (2) the presentation of the women characters in the context of a possibly redemptive 'love'.

Swift has a stated predilection for first-person narration: 'I actually think the first person is more fertile – you can throw attention on to the person who is narrating as much as on to the story'; 'Writing in the first person is a complete act of imagination. Once I have invented characters I find that I have immediate, internal access to them. I see through their eyes'.[1] This suggests a very close identification between author and narrator, albeit one in which the author speaks *as* character rather than – as one might more commonly expect – the character speaking *for* the author. Certainly we can readily 'characterize' each of Swift's narrators: Willy Chapman as uxurious and self-deprecating shopkeeper; Prentis, in the shadow of his father and his boss, as insecure petty domestic tyrant; Tom Crick as unfulfilled and demoralized schoolteacher, ironically trapped both by his past and by his belief in history; Harry Beech as hard-bitten photo-journalist softening up through age and love, and Sophie as a 'fucked-up' child of violence and emotional deprivation; Bill Unwin as pseudo-don, Prufrock-like Hamlet and incorrigible romantic; the Bermondsey 'pilgrims' as (sharply differentiated) small-time failures in life and love; George Webb as yet another failure in profession and relationships, now besotted by a gaoled murderess he barely knows. All of them, then, come across as distinctively realized characters who are not Swift.

But what is unusual is that there seems to be little indication in the texture of the novels that the narrators are in fact 'unreliable narrators' as usually understood in critical terminology (that is, those strategically angled to reveal themselves as 'untrustworthy' without being conscious of it). It does not appear, in other words, that they are subjected to that kind of authorial or structural irony as part of the novels' overall project. The problem, if such it is, with this absence of an ironic gap between author and narrator is that the reader has little with which to judge the credibility or veracity of the 'his-story' being narrated. While we may discern the nastiness of Prentis in the first half of *Shuttlecock*, and therefore take this into account when assessing his narrative, the 'focalization' technique in *The Sweet Shop Owner* means that the story bounced off Willy's consciousness constitutes the absolute parameters of what we know. And while, as I have suggested, George in *The Light of Day* is perhaps Swift's only truly unreliable narrator, in that we can see round the edges of his narrative and establish a different perspective to judge his world from than the one he believes he is conveying, this is not the case with Tom Crick, Harry Beech (albeit framed by the other narrators), Bill Unwin and Ray Johnson, whose narratives we are not in a position to challenge because they are the more or less 'straight' source of all our information. For example, while Crick and the reader know that salvaging 'the whole story' from the murky and unstable terrain of the past is impossible, how are we to judge his other views about history, curiosity, civilization, progress, and so on? Does the novel not then seem to confirm them? So that, although the author may be 'in character' as the narrative voice, there is precious little opportunity to circumvent that voice; hence the character does indeed appear to be speaking for the author – or, at the very least, the author seems to be endorsing what the narrator is telling us. The description of the adolescent Mary in *Waterland* is a case in point:

> It was she whose fingers first got the itch and were at work before I dared, and only then at her prompting – her grabbing and guiding of my hand [...] to use mine.
>
> Mary itched. And this itch of Mary's was the itch of curiosity. In

110

her fifteen-year-old body curiosity tickled and chafed, making her fidgety and roving-eyed. Curiosity drove her, beyond all restraint, to want to touch, witness, experience whatever was unknown and hidden from her. (*W*. 51)

While it is clear that it is Tom reminiscing in the first paragraph, whose is that authoritative voice in the second anatomizing Mary's 'itch'? Whose is it making the judgments 'roving-eyed' and 'beyond all restraint'? Whose is it that propounds the virtues of 'curiosity' throughout the novel, and who seems to condemn Mary for her loss of it? The problem is that we cannot quite tell: certainly it is Tom, but is it also Tom with the author behind him?

The kind of problem that may arise from this uncertain distinction between author and narrative voice may be seen in the second of the two unresolved issues that Swift's novels raise for me: love and their women characters. While the importance of love is continuously *stated* throughout the novels, an inverse index of this, as we have seen, is its ubiquitous absence in Swift's wasteland, where there is a powerful sense of the *failure* of love – lovelessness between men and women and between parents and children (childlessness is also frequently symptomatic). Let us take stock of the principal characters' relationships: Willy Chapman, forbidden to love his wife and estranged from his daughter; Prentis's alienating relations with his wife and sons; the drift of Tom and Mary Crick's marriage into childless and sterile routine; the death of Harry Beech's unfaithful wife, Anna, in an air crash, and his estrangement from his daughter Sophie; Bill and Ruth Unwin's discovery of 'the real thing', but which ends with her suicide after a childless marriage; Jack, Amy and their brain-damaged daughter, Ray and Lenny and their estranged daughters; Sarah Nash's murder of her husband, and George's hopeless infatuation with her thereafter. Even the minute signs of possible redemption through love are only ever tentative and oblique: either they are posited as abstractions (Tom Crick's equation of 'curiosity' and 'love'; Bill Unwin's celebration of 'romantic love'), or as *memories* of desire and fulfilment (Bill and Ruth's 'first night of bliss' in the late 1950s; Ray and Amy in the camper van during their affair in 1967), or as unrealized (and fragile) possibilities beyond the limits of the novel (Harry Beech and the pregnant Jenny, Harry reconciled with Sophie; Ray and Amy and the visit to Australia; George and Sarah when she is finally released into 'the light of day'). The *possibility* of love, then – combined with the process of exploring the past through [hi]stories in order to 'explain' how these modern lives have become so wasted – seems to be the minimalist solution to the otherwise sterile and futureless 'Here and Now'.

But what may have become apparent from the synoptic overview above is that these 'his-stories' – and with very few exceptions that is indeed what they are – either silence women or present them unfavourably. While *de facto*, as 'his-stories', women are not given a voice, this seems to be emblematized by the number of female characters who literally become silenced physically and/or institutionally (Sarah Atkinson and Mary in *Waterland*, the dead Anna in *Out of This World*, Ruth and Sylvia in *Ever After*, June in *Last Orders*, Sarah in *The Light of Day*). But all the women characters are also 'silent' in the sense that they remain undeveloped as autonomous individuals, being mediated to us exclusively through the male narrative discourse (Dorothy Chapman, Marian Prentis, Mary Metcalf, Anna Beech, Sarah Nash, Kristina Lazic – even the wonderfully talented and charismatic actress, Ruth Unwin). Furthermore, in many cases they are the villains of the piece, responsible for whatever damage has been done – usually by being sexually promiscuous. We may recall Mary's teenage sexual 'curiosity' and the results that flow from that (including her own loss of this and later insanity – as punishment?); that Anna Beech goes to bed with a friend of Harry's and is shortly afterwards killed in a plane crash (punishment?), while Sophie 'fucks around. Your Dad is good about things. Because he's good, she fucks' (*OTW* 39); Sylvia Unwin is a 'bitch' (*EA* 196) whose torrid affair with Sam may have caused her husband's suicide (that or knowledge of her earlier affair with Bill's 'real' father), and she dies of throat cancer; Ray Johnson's wife deserts him for another man, and Amy Dodds has an affair with him, her husband's best friend; Kristina seduces Bob Nash away from Sarah, who then stabs him to death with a kitchen knife and is once again locked away in an institution.

What I want to suggest, therefore, is that even the proposed potentially redemptive power of love in Swift's novels is undercut by a feature of its actual textual realization, in that the treatment of the female characters seems to me to be problematic by apparently failing to break free from some very conventional male sexual attitudes towards women. In *Last Orders*, Vince describes making love with Mandy in the camper van: 'I liked it cramped and squashed and hasty [...] *and I reckon that's how she liked it, too*, because it didn't take much coaxing [...]' (*LO* 103; emphasis added). And George in *The Light of Day*, speculating that Bob and Kristina have sex on Wimbledon Common (why? is this a pertinent aspect of his character?), also seems to know what a woman 'likes': 'An extra thrill. They might have fucked against a tree [...] *Part of her wants it, likes it like that*' (*LD* 59; emphasis added). But it is here, of course, that my first 'problem' – with the ambiguous status of Swift's first-person male narrators – relates to the second (the redemptive power of 'love'), for are we to assume that the sexist representations of women outlined above are strictly and solely those of the novels' narrators? But there is seldom an occasion when the reader feels the narrators' attitudes are indeed being set up for and with ironic distaste.This peculiarly male way of thinking about sex is, however, even more obtrusive when the women characters *are* given a voice in the occasional sections they narrate. Mandy's own version of camper-van sex, for instance, sounds suspiciously similar to Vince's: 'I felt his cock stiffening under my hand.[...] He rolled me over and shoved into me and I lifted my knees and gripped him' (*LO* 160). And Sophie in *Out of This World* describes seducing a plumber in New York as a young wife as follows:

I [...] stood nearer so he could look at my legs.[...] He got up [...] I put my hand on his cock, hard as a pistol, and he hitched up my skirt, right here in this kitchen, with his hands greasy, with the twins upstairs sleeping, and I said, 'C'mon! C'mon fuck me, fuck me good, you great hog!' (*OTW* 18)

Certainly it is part of her 'fucked-up' character to go in for 'cheap, quick, mindless screws' (*OTW* 96), but that is not the issue: the point, rather, is the *manner* in which she describes them. But the effect of such prurient discourse is to make the already uncertain and vulnerable positive of 'love' even less convincing as an antidote to the postmodern malaise than it is in the conscious schema of the novels. For if love is only posited in generalized, abstract and one-sided terms, and rendered by a conception of sex that seems to owe its provenance to male fantasy, then redemption solely by 'his-stories' appears to be a forlorn hope. The fact that there are no true 'her-stories' in Swift's otherwise sophisticated and perceptive fiction perhaps suggests that a dimension missing from it is one provided by the women's movement from the 1960s onwards, which has promoted the need for public and personal political endeavour based on mutual respect and understanding between the sexes as a means of displacing the dehumanizing stasis at the heart of postmodern societies.

I began this conclusion by proposing that a contemporary literary work is grounded in the world in which it is written and read, and to which its version of that world alludes. A 'politics of reading', then, requires the reader to identify the social and cultural contexts in which the text locates itself, and to evaluate the stances it takes to them. Graham Swift's metafiction, I have suggested, at once offers a historical explanation (from the First and Second World Wars at least) for the nature of late-twentieth-century British society, represents its (postmodern) features in a chilling light, and implies that salvation is possible only if we retain some vestiges of a humanism in which reclaiming the past ('telling [hi]stories') and 'love' are central. These are the contexts that are woven into the text, and the way they are presented enunciates the text's own politics. The reader's task is to identify and assess the latter. And if we find that the only politics present are a tacit politics of no politics (a wistful and dispirited invocation of 'love'), does this point us paradoxically towards other forms of politics that the novels occlude – politics in which collective human action seeks to promote change and to replace anomie with agency and accountability? Or is this implied request for solutions simply asking too much of a novelist – whose craft, after all, is principally to hold up a finely polished looking glass for us to see how we are, rather than how we should be?

Notes

INTRODUCTION

1. John O'Mahony, 'Triumph of the Common Man', *Guardian*, 'Saturday Review', 1 Mar. 2003, p. 22.
2. First quotation from an address given at the International Writers' Union, 1988; second quotation from an interview with E. Jane Dickson, *Sunday Times*, 1992. Both reproduced in *LS* 218–19, 'Resource Notes'.
3. *Guardian*, 1 Mar. 2003, p. 22.
4. Ibid. 22.
5. Professor Hugh Haughton, University of York, in ibid.
6. Graham Swift, '1974', in *21 Picador Authors Celebrate 21 Years of International Writing* (London and Basingstoke: Pan Books (Picador), 1993), 21, 25.
7. Linda Hutcheon, *The Politics of Postmodernism* (1989; 2nd edn., New Accents; London and New York: Routledge, 2002), 7, 14.
8. Ibid. 51–4.
9. James Green, 'The Sense of a (Non-)Ending: Ending and Endings in British Fiction of the 1980s and '90s', undergraduate dissertation (University of Gloucestershire, May 2003), 47–8.
10. Hutcheon, *The Politics of Postmodernism*, 13.
11. Christopher Isherwood, 'Foreword' to Edward Upward's short story, 'The Railway Accident', in *New Directions in Prose and Poetry: Number Eleven* (New York, 1949), reproduced in Edward Upward, *The Railway Accident and Other Stories* (1969; Harmondsworth: Penguin Books, 1972), 34.

CHAPTER 1. EARLY NOVELS: *THE SWEET SHOP OWNER* AND *SHUTTLECOCK*

1. William Shakespeare, *King Lear*, ed. Kenneth Muir (The Arden

Shakespeare; London: Methuen, 1963), Act III, Scene iv, ll. 28–36.
2. Ibid., ll. 105–12.

CHAPTER 2. *WATERLAND*

1. Raymond Williams, *Keywords* (London: Fontana/Croom Helm, 1976), 119.
2. Ibid.
3. Martin Amis, 'Thinkability', introductory essay to *Einstein's Monsters* (1987; Harmondsworth: Penguin, 1988), 17.
4. T. S. Eliot, 'Burnt Norton', in *Four Quartets* (1943; London: Faber, 1959), 14.
5. Thomas Carlyle, 'On History' (1830), in Alan Shelston (ed.), *Thomas Carlyle: Selected Writings* (Harmondsworth: Penguin Books, 1971).

CHAPTER 3. *OUT OF THIS WORLD*

1. Jean Baudrillard, 'The Reality Gulf', *Guardian*, 11 Jan. 1991, and *The Gulf War Did Not Take Place*, trans. Paul Patton (London: Power Publications, 1995).
2. 'Preface to *The Spoils of Poynton*' (1907), in Henry James, *The Art of the Novel: Critical Prefaces* (New York and London: Charles Scribner's Sons, 1962), 122.

CHAPTER 4. *EVER AFTER*

1. Alfred, Lord Tennyson, *In Memoriam* (1850), xcvi.
2. E. M. Forster, *Maurice* (written 1913; 1971; Harmondsworth: Penguin Books, 1975), 218.

CHAPTER 5. *LAST ORDERS*

1. The date is established at *LO*. 272.
2. Less than six months after *Last Orders* had won the Booker Prize, John Frow, Professor of English at the University of Queensland, wrote a letter to the *Australian*'s 'Review of Books' pointing out that Swift's novel was 'almost identical' to Faulkner's 'without acknowledgement'. This was reported, *inter alia*, in the *Guardian* (10 Mar. 1997) and the *Independent on Sunday* (16 Mar. 1997), causing a furious

response, mainly by supporters of Swift.

3. Quoted in the *Guardian* and in a letter to the *Independent on Sunday* (see n. 2 above).

4. T. S. Eliot, *The Waste Land*, in *Collected Poems, 1909–1962* (London: Faber & Faber, 1963), ll. 1–7. References *passim* to Eliot's poem in the pages that follow here are to this edition.

CHAPTER 6. *THE LIGHT OF DAY*

1. Hermione Lee, 'Someone to watch over you', 'Book of the week', *Guardian* 'Saturday Review', 8 Mar. 2003, p. 9.

2. Quoted in John O'Mahony, 'Triumph of the Common Man', *Guardian*, 'Saturday Review', 1 Mar. 2003, p. 22.

3. Quoted without source in Martin Seymour-Smith, *The Macmillan Guide to Modern World Literature* (1973; Basingstoke: Macmillan, 1985), 275.

4. Boyd Tonkin, 'Distant voices, still lives', *Independent* 'Magazine', Mar. 2003, p. 19.

5. E. M. Forster, *Howards End* (1910; Harmondsworth: Penguin Books, 1961), 316.

CONCLUSION

1. First quotation from an interview with Thomas Sutcliffe in *Independent*, 1988; second quotation from an interview with E. Jane Dickson, *Sunday Times*, 1992. Both reproduced in *LS* 218–19: 'Resource Notes'.

Select Bibliography

WORKS BY GRAHAM SWIFT

Learning to Swim and Other Stories (London: London Magazine Editions, 1982), ed. with introduction and notes by Richard Hoyes (Cambridge Literature edn.; Cambridge: Cambridge University Press, 1995).

The Sweet Shop Owner (London: Allen Lane, 1980; Harmondsworth: Penguin Books, 1983).

Shuttlecock (London: Allen Lane, 1981; Harmondsworth: Penguin Books, 1982).

Waterland (London: William Heinemann, 1983; paperback edn., London: Picador, 1984; rev. paperback edn., London: Picador, 1992).

Out of This World (London: Viking, 1988: Harmondsworth: Penguin Books, 1988).

Ever After (London: Pan Books, 1992; London: Picador, 1992).

Last Orders (London: Picador, 1996; London: Picador, 2001).

The Light of Day (London: Hamish Hamilton, 2003; London: Penguin Books, 2004).

CRITICAL STUDIES

Brewer, John, and Tillyard, Stella, 'History and Telling Stories: Graham Swift's *Waterland*', *History Today*, 35 (Jan. 1985), 49–51. Perceptive comments on Tom Crick as narrator and on 'nature' versus 'history'.

Cooper, Pamela, 'Imperial Topographies: The Spaces of History in *Waterland*', *Modern Fiction Studies*, 42/2 (Summer 1996), 371–96.

—— *Graham Swift's* Last Orders: *A Reader's Guide* (New York and London: Continuum 'Contemporaries', 2002).

Gasiorek, Andrzej, *Post-War British Fiction: Realism and After* (London:

Edward Arnold, 1995). Part of chapter 7, 'Postmodernism and the Problem of History', discusses how *Waterland* positions itself in relation to nineteenth-century views of 'History' (principally those of Carlyle and Kant).

Green, James, 'The Sense of a (Non-)Ending: Ending and Endings in British Fiction of the 1980s and '90s', undergraduate dissertation (University of Gloucestershire, May 2003).

Higdon, David Leon, ' "Unconfessed Confessions": The Narrators of Julian Barnes and Graham Swift', in James Acheson (ed.), *The British and Irish Novel since 1960* (Basingstoke: Macmillan, 1991).

Hutcheon, Linda, *The Politics of Postmodernism* (1989; 2nd edn., New Accents; London and New York: Routledge, 2002). Good general introduction to postmodernist representation and to what Hutcheon terms 'historiographic metafiction' (part of chapter 2 uses *Waterland* as an example, pp. 51–4).

Janik, Del Ivan, 'History and the "Here and Now": The Novels of Graham Swift', *Twentieth-Century Literature*, 35/1 (Spring 1989), 74–88.

Landow, George P., 'History, His Story, and Stories in Graham Swift's *Waterland*', *Studies in the Literary Imagination*, 23 (1990), 197–211.

Malcolm, David, *Understanding Graham Swift* (Columbia SC: University of South Carolina Press, 2003). Published after the final draft of my own book was completed, this is a comprehensive introduction to all of Graham Swift's fiction to date.

Schad, John, 'The End of the End of History: Graham Swift's *Waterland*', *Modern Fiction Studies*, 38/4 (Winter 1992), 911–25.

119

Index

Recent and Forthcoming Titles in the New Series of

WRITERS AND THEIR WORK

"... this series promises to outshine its own
previously high reputation."
Times Higher Education Supplement

"...will build into a fine multi-volume critical
encyclopaedia of English literature."
Library Review & Reference Review

"...Excellent, informative, readable, and recommended."
NATE News

"written by outstanding contemporary critics,
whose expertise is flavoured by unashamed enthusiasm for
their subjects and the series' diverse aspirations."
Times Educational Supplement

"A useful and timely addition to the ranks of the lit crit and
reviews genre. Written in an accessible and authoritative style."
Library Association Record

WRITERS AND THEIR WORK

RECENT & FORTHCOMING TITLES

Title	Author
Chinua Achebe	*Nahem Yousaf*
Peter Ackroyd	*Susana Onega*
Kingsley Amis	*Richard Bradford*
Anglo-Saxon Verse	*Graham Holderness*
Antony and Cleopatra 2/e	*Ken Parker*
As You Like It	*Penny Gay*
W. H. Auden	*Stan Smith*
Jane Austen	*Robert Miles*
Alan Ayckbourn	*Michael Holt*
J. G. Ballard	*Michel Delville*
Pat Barker	*Sharon Monteith*
Djuna Barnes	*Deborah Parsons*
Julian Barnes	*Matthew Pateman*
Samuel Beckett	*Sinead Mooney*
Aphra Behn 2/e	*S. J. Wiseman*
John Betjeman	*Dennis Brown*
William Blake	*Steven Vine*
Edward Bond	*Michael Mangan*
Anne Brontë	*Betty Jay*
Emily Brontë	*Stevie Davies*
Robert Browning	*John Woodford*
A. S. Byatt	*Richard Todd*
Byron	*Drummond Bone*
Caroline Drama	*Julie Sanders*
Angela Carter 2/e	*Lorna Sage*
Bruce Chatwin	*Kerry Featherstone*
Geoffrey Chaucer	*Steve Ellis*
Children's Literature	*Kimberley Reynolds*
Children's Writers of the 19th Century	*Mary Sebag-Montefiore*
Caryl Churchill 2/e	*Elaine Aston*
John Clare	*John Lucas*
S. T. Coleridge	*Stephen Bygrave*
Joseph Conrad	*Cedric Watts*
Coriolanus	*Anita Pacheco*
Stephen Crane	*Kevin Hayes*
Crime Fiction	*Martin Priestman*
Anita Desai	*Elaine Ho*
Shashi Deshpande	*Amrita Bhalla*
Charles Dickens	*Rod Mengham*
John Donne	*Stevie Davies*
Margaret Drabble	*Glenda Leeming*
John Dryden	*David Hopkins*
Carol Ann Duffy 2/e	*Deryn Rees Jones*
Early Modern Sonneteers	*Michael Spiller*
George Eliot	*Josephine McDonagh*
T. S. Eliot	*Colin MacCabe*
English Translators of Homer	*Simeon Underwood*
Henry Fielding	*Jenny Uglow*
Veronica Forrest-Thomson – Language Poetry	*Alison Mark*
E. M. Forster	*Nicholas Royle*

Title	Author
John Fowles	*William Stephenson*
Brian Friel	*Geraldine Higgins*
Athol Fugard	*Dennis Walder*
Elizabeth Gaskell	*Kate Flint*
The *Gawain*-Poet	*John Burrow*
The Georgian Poets	*Rennie Parker*
William Golding 2/e	*Kevin McCarron*
Graham Greene	*Peter Mudford*
Neil M. Gunn	*J. B. Pick*
Ivor Gurney	*John Lucas*
Hamlet 2/e	*Ann Thompson & Neil Taylor*
Thomas Hardy 2/e	*Peter Widdowson*
Tony Harrison	*Joe Kelleher*
William Hazlitt	*J. B. Priestley; R. L. Brett (intro. by Michael Foot)*
Seamus Heaney 2/e	*Andrew Murphy*
George Herbert	*T.S. Eliot (intro. by Peter Porter)*
Geoffrey Hill	*Andrew Roberts*
Gerard Manley Hopkins	*Daniel Brown*
Henrik Ibsen 2/e	*Sally Ledger*
Kazuo Ishiguro 2/e	*Cynthia Wong*
Henry James – The Later Writing	*Barbara Hardy*
James Joyce 2/e	*Steven Connor*
Julius Caesar	*Mary Hamer*
Franz Kafka	*Michael Wood*
John Keats	*Kelvin Everest*
James Kelman	*Gustav Klaus*
Hanif Kureishi	*Ruvani Ranasinha*
Samuel Johnson	*Liz Bellamy*
William Langland: *Piers Plowman*	*Claire Marshall*
King Lear	*Terence Hawkes*
Philip Larkin 2/e	*Laurence Lerner*
D. H. Lawrence	*Linda Ruth Williams*
Doris Lessing	*Elizabeth Maslen*
C. S. Lewis	*William Gray*
Wyndham Lewis and Modernism	*Andrzej Gasiorak*
David Lodge	*Bernard Bergonzi*
Katherine Mansfield	*Andrew Bennett*
Christopher Marlowe	*Thomas Healy*
Andrew Marvell	*Annabel Patterson*
Ian McEwan 2/e	*Kiernan Ryan*
Measure for Measure	*Kate Chedgzoy*
The Merchant of Venice	*Warren Chernaik*
A Midsummer Night's Dream	*Helen Hackett*
Alice Munro	*Ailsa Cox*
Vladimir Nabokov	*Neil Cornwell*
V. S. Naipaul	*Suman Gupta*
Grace Nichols	*Sarah Lawson-Welsh*
Edna O'Brien	*Amanda Greenwood*
Flann O'Brien	*Joe Brooker*
Ben Okri	*Robert Fraser*
George Orwell	*Douglas Kerr*
Othello	*Emma Smith*
Walter Pater	*Laurel Brake*

RECENT & FORTHCOMING TITLES

TITLES IN PREPARATION

Title	Author
Fleur Adcock	*Janet Wilson*
Ama Ata Aidoo	*Nana Wilson-Tagoe*
Matthew Arnold	*Kate Campbell*
Margaret Atwood	*Marion Wynne-Davies*
John Banville	*Peter Dempsey*
William Barnes	*Christopher Ricks*
Black British Writers	*Deidre Osborne*
Charlotte Brontë	*Stevie Davies*
Basil Bunting	*Martin Stannard*
John Bunyan	*Tamsin Spargoe*
Cymbeline	*Peter Swaab*
Douglas Dunn	*David Kennedy*
David Edgar	*Peter Boxall*
J. G. Farrell	*John McLeod*
Nadine Gordimer	*Lewis Nkosi*
Geoffrey Grigson	*R. M. Healey*
David Hare	*Jeremy Ridgman*
Ted Hughes	*Susan Bassnett*
The Imagist Poets	*Andrew Thacker*
Ben Jonson	*Anthony Johnson*
A. L. Kennedy	*Dorothy McMillan*
Jack Kerouac	*Michael Hrebebiak*
Jamaica Kincaid	*Susheila Nasta*
Rudyard Kipling	*Jan Montefiore*
Rosamond Lehmann	*Judy Simon*
Una Marson & Louise Bennett	*Alison Donnell*
Norman MacCaig	*Alasdair Macrae*
Thomas Middleton	*Hutchings & Bromham*
John Milton	*Nigel Smith*
Much Ado About Nothing	*John Wilders*
R. K. Narayan	*Shirley Chew*
New Woman Writers	*Marion Shaw/Lyssa Randolph*
Ngugi wa Thiong'o	*Brendon Nicholls*
Religious Poets of the 17th Century	*Helen Wilcox*
Samuel Richardson	*David Deeming*
Olive Schreiner	*Carolyn Burdett*
Sam Selvon	*Ramchand & Salick*
Olive Senior	*Denise de Canes Narain*
Mary Shelley	*Catherine Sharrock*
Charlotte Smith & Helen Williams	*Angela Keane*
R. L. Stevenson	*David Robb*
Tom Stoppard	*Nicholas Cadden*
Elizabeth Taylor	*N. R. Reeve*
Dylan Thomas	*Chris Wiggington*
Three Avant-Garde Poets	*Peter Middleton*
Three Lyric Poets	*William Rowe*
Derek Walcott	*Stephen Regan*
Jeanette Winterson	*Gina Vitello*
Women's Poetry at the Fin de Siècle	*Anna Vadillo*
William Wordsworth	*Nicola Trott*